533 A.D.

Roman Emperor Justinian included Rhodian sea law in recodification of statutes drawn up to govern far-flung empire

1288

English Guild of Blessed Mary withheld fire insurance benefits from persons guilty of "lust, dice-playing, and gluttony"

1347

Earliest known complete contract of insurance, covering voyage of ship "Santa Clara" was recorded at Port of Genoa, Italy

1574

Queen Elizabeth signed bill which established "Chamber of Insurance" designed to provide protection facilities for shippers

continued on back end lining

Risks We Face

Risks We Face

AN INTRODUCTION TO PROPERTY INSURANCE

New and revised edition, August, 1956

Original edition, 1944, edited by

LAURENCE J. ACKERMAN

Dean, School of Business Administration
University of Connecticut

and

RALPH W. BUGLI

formerly National Board of Fire Underwriters

Appreciation is expressed to Laurence J. Ackerman for his helpful comments in this revised edition

NATIONAL BOARD OF FIRE UNDERWRITERS

New York   San Francisco   Chicago

Every property owner faces the chance of loss due to fire and to many other perils beyond his control.

Property insurance provides the means by which relatively small sums are paid by many persons in order to meet losses suffered by the unfortunate few. Through insurance the property owner substitutes the certainty of a small payment for the uncertainty of a large loss.

This book explains the various risks people face and how insurance companies handle those risks for them.

44-7419

Introduction

Risks We Face is designed to give the reader a brief, non-technical survey of property insurance not only as an important element of our economic life but as it relates to the individual personally and in business.

There has been a need for a manual written for the layman and the student that would be helpful in the problems facing not only those in business and industry but every home-dweller as well. *Risks We Face* has been designed to fill this need. Fire insurance is basic but property insurance also includes windstorm, hail, automobile, inland marine, burglary and similar types of insurance.

Teachers of economics, home economics, general business and social science courses on the collegiate or high school level, dealing with the topic of property insurance, have called for something more comprehensive than the very brief treatment found in the usual college or high school text. They want material more extensive in its treatment of property insurance, and at the same time sufficiently simple to be effective with students. Also, insurance agencies and insurance companies, in meeting the problem of inducting new personnel into their organizations, have sought some simple presentation to introduce the business to these people. It is hoped that the book will also serve other groups, such as adult study classes, business and consumer organizations, buyers and those who, in their work, can utilize a general approach to property insurance.

This revised second edition brings the excellent, original text up to date so that it accurately reflects the changes in

v

the business that have taken place in the swiftly moving economic scene in the ten years since the first edition.

The text opens with the explanation of the vital importance of property insurance to the nation and stresses that property insurance is the foundation stone of the whole credit system. It then sketches briefly the origin and development of insurance practices to meet the various uncertainties that are the generating force creating the necessity for insurance and proceeds to describe property insurance in action today. Types of insurance organizations, the contracts they issue, and the role of the local insurance representatives are described. Fire prevention as an important function of the property insurance business is discussed in relative detail. The significance of property insurance to the community and to the individual concludes the discussion.

Many volumes would be required to tell the full story of any enterprise as far-reaching in effect and as interesting in detail as property insurance. *Risks We Face* is not a manual of technical details. These details the advanced student may, if he wishes, find in a number of excellent texts.* The editors have sought throughout to select and present concise factual material that will help the reader to form a clear general picture of the business and to obtain an understanding of its economic importance.

So many educational and insurance leaders have helped make possible both the original edition and the present revision that the editor's sincere thanks must go to all.

It is hoped that *Risks We Face* may help increase the reader's understanding of how closely the business of property insurance concerns our daily economic life and how the property insurance business helps to safeguard the security and peace of mind of the typical citizen.

---

* See Reading List, Appendix C, page 111.

Table of Contents

APPENDICES

"If I had my way, I would write the word *insurance* over the door of every cottage and upon the blotting book of every public man, because I am convinced that for sacrifices which are inconceivably small, families can be secured against catastrophes which would smash them forever."

WINSTON CHURCHILL

1

How Property Insurance
Serves The Nation

Have you ever stopped to consider the peace of mind and security you enjoy when you are safeguarded by insurance against the financial hazards we face daily?

Property insurance has in recent years become one of our basic institutions, ranking with banking, transportation and communications in its significance to the home and to business. This was not always so. At the turn of the century it was not unusual to hear of some important businessman who had lost everything when his store or factory had been wiped out by fire or one of the many other hazards faced by industry. He did not believe in insurance or considered insurance rates too high and had therefore taken a chance. Property insurance has become a part of the very fabric of our civilization and culture and is considered virtually indispensable to our present economic system. Today, no sensible businessman would consider for a moment foregoing the benefits of its protection, and the homeowner who does not carry property insurance is considered foolhardy.

Property insurance has done much to encourage the marvelous growth of industry, of which America is so justly proud, by lifting the important burden of risk from those who would pioneer in new ventures. For example, in aviation, television, and other rapidly developing industries, there are sufficient uncertainties without the additional risks of destruction of property by fire or similar perils. In practically every form of business enterprise, sound insurance protection has been an encouragement to the investment of capital in the face of these additional risks.

Property insurance protects the manufacturer, the merchant, and the buyer of goods and services. If there were no insurance, the average businessman would have to charge more—for the food we eat, for the clothes we wear, and for the products we use—in order to try to safeguard himself against unpredictable losses. If each businessman attempted to provide these safeguards himself, the venture would be less efficient and more costly than it is through group action.

Property insurance has stimulated as well as kept pace with the tremendous growth of the nation's resources and productive plant. New types of insurance protection have moved swiftly into the picture as the needs of the nation have grown. Insurance has remained highly sensitive to the needs of individuals and businesses for protection. It stands ready and eager to provide its special service in the form that is most desirable and useful to its policyholders.

Foundation Stone of Credit System

Property insurance is a foundation stone of our modern credit system under which most homes, cars, and other substantial purchases are financed today. When property subject to destruction by fire or other hazards forms the basis for a loan, few bankers today will extend credit unless insurance is carried as protection for the loan. Few homeowners would be permitted to buy houses with only a small cash payment unless the lending institution providing the necessary balance of purchase money could protect itself through insurance.

In establishing credit, assets must be backed by insurance

Property insurance is an important investor in American progress. The dollars that represent the capital stock, the surplus, and the unearned premium reserve of an insurance company are essentially "double duty dollars." Besides serving as the financial guardians of each policy-holder's property, these dollars are put to additional full-time work. They are invested in hundreds of other industries, permitting these businesses to grow and expand. Insurance companies select for the investment of their funds the soundest types of ventures, choosing them from every section of the country and from many types of industries so that local depressions or catastrophes will not endanger them.

Recognizing that the United States Government is one of the soundest ventures for any investor, property insurance companies have consistently invested in government bonds, in time of peace as well as war. In the investment portfolios of many companies, government bonds represent a large

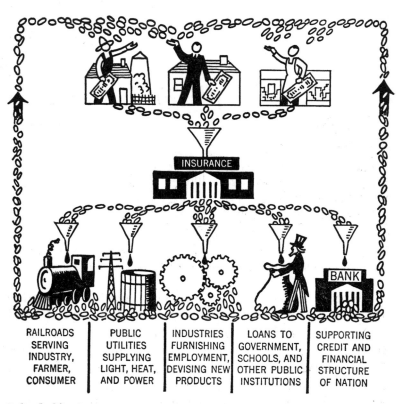

| RAILROADS SERVING INDUSTRY, FARMER, CONSUMER | PUBLIC UTILITIES SUPPLYING LIGHT, HEAT, AND POWER | INDUSTRIES FURNISHING EMPLOYMENT, DEVISING NEW PRODUCTS | LOANS TO GOVERNMENT, SCHOOLS, AND OTHER PUBLIC INSTITUTIONS | SUPPORTING CREDIT AND FINANCIAL STRUCTURE OF NATION |

Policyholders' premiums are "double-duty dollars". Providing protection against financial loss, they are at the same time at work in the nation's daily life.

individual item; state and municipal bonds are also included therein.

Insurance in Peace and War

In peacetime, insurance is a pillar of the economic structure of the nation. In wartime, it takes on a special responsibility. Through its trained prevention and protection engineers, it helps to safeguard from fire and other hazards hundreds of camps, barracks, navy yards, industrial and war plants and waterfront properties. It reduces the element of risk in the operations of thousands of businessmen engaged in producing and delivering the sinews of war. It constantly impresses upon the public the reminder that every fire which diverts men and materials from war work is as destructive as sabotage.

Insurance is a cushion against disaster, a shock absorber that makes it possible to face some of life's catastrophes and to survive them with a minimum of hardship. When an insurance agent or broker sells a policy, the transaction means much more than an ordinary sale of merchandise. It means that a promise of protection has been delivered and that security has been extended to another home, another industry, another community.

2
Meeting Uncertainty

The most certain thing confronting individuals and institutions is uncertainty. This is the basic reason for all types of insurance. No one can escape constant exposure to a variety of perils. Each day we face the possibility that something unexpected may disturb the normal tenor of our living. High winds damage or destroy homes. Burglars may steal valuable possessions. Serious accidents may cause hospitalization. Fire may destroy real and personal property of every description. The problem of dealing with these constant perils is one of the most important factors in modern living.

We all face two types of perils: group perils and individual perils. Group perils are those over which we have practically no control. A war and its consequences, for example, represent a group peril which may affect us seriously, but there is little that we, as individuals, can do about it.

Individual perils are essentially personal. As individuals, we have some degree of control over their origin. For instance, the peril of loss as a result of fire is an individual peril. By observing simple fire prevention rules, a property owner can do much to reduce and control fire hazards.

Not all the types of perils to which property is exposed will be discussed in detail in this introduction to property insurance. A specific kind of individual peril, the chance of loss resulting from the destruction of property due to fire, to the forces of nature, and to similar causes, will be discussed here.

Meeting the Peril of Fire

Consider the constant peril of fire, for example. Despite our knowledge of fire prevention methods, fire each year destroys thousands of lives and hundreds of millions of dollars' worth of property in the United States.

What can a person do about this peril?

The individual might choose to do nothing. But that could prove to be a costly gamble, and would be evading the problem, not solving it. He might decide to create and build up a savings fund to prepare for the financial shock of a possible fire loss. This method might be satisfactory if no immediate loss occurred. But there is no guarantee that a property owner will be so fortunate.

The problem can be handled best through a third alternative—a combination of risk analysis and insurance protection, with first consideration given to the magnitude and importance of the hazards involved. The individual could proceed to handle the perils to his property in the following manner:

1. He can survey the risks to which he is exposed. "Is there a chance of loss from fire, windstorm, explosion, hail, and so forth?" This survey should determine every chance of a major loss.

2. His risks surveyed and appraised, he can reduce or eliminate the obvious causes of loss. For example, if the property owner has been careless in handling flammable materials, he can reduce the risk of a disastrous fire from that cause by installing special containers in which to store paints, volatile oils, and similar products.

Naturally, he should not stop after eliminating such an obvious cause of loss but should continue to seek out and remove every possible fire hazard on his property.

Even after the property owner has appraised his risks, has reduced some and eliminated others, there remains an irreducible minimum of risk over which he has no control. The individual, for example, has no control over a fire that originates in his neighbor's home and spreads throughout the community. Since the chance of loss due to fire can never be eliminated completely, a third step in dealing with perils to property becomes necessary.

3. The individual can transfer the remaining chance of loss to a professional risk-bearer—an insurance organization—by purchasing an insurance policy.

The operations that make it possible for an insurance company to transform this piece of paper called a policy into payments of money when losses occur represent one of the most interesting aspects of modern business.

SURVEYING RISKS

REDUCING RISKS

TRANSFERRING RISKS

The Law of Large Numbers

The foundation upon which insurance rests is the law of large numbers, popularly known as the law of averages. Experience has shown that a certain number out of a given group of properties will be destroyed by fire and other perils. The larger the group of individual properties exposed to the chance of loss, the greater the accuracy with which the approximate number of future losses can be predicted.

LAW OF
LARGE
NUMBERS

While experience shows how many fires may be expected in a typical large group of properties in a given period, no one can predict which properties or which small groups will have no fires

This principle can be demonstrated by the simple operation of tossing a penny into the air. If you flip long enough, the result will be an equal number of "heads" and "tails." If you try only ten times, the result is likely to be much less accurate than if you try a hundred or a thousand times. At no time during your experiment will you be able to predict definitely that either a "head" or a "tail" will appear on any given toss.

While experience shows how many fires may be expected in a typical large group of properties in a given period, no one can predict which properties or which small groups will have no fires.

Insurance men know from experience that if they issue policies covering a large enough group of properties, they can estimate closely the number and amount of the losses they will normally pay. Thus they are able to determine how much must be paid by policyholders to cover losses and operating costs.

This fact explains why an insurance company can promise to pay a relatively large sum of money in the event of loss although the policyholder has paid only a comparatively small amount to the company for taking the risk.

Insurance Not a Wager

Insurance is the direct opposite of gambling. In gambling, there is no risk until you wager. In Insurance the risk is always present. Sometimes one says he is betting with the insurance company against the contingency of his house burning. If it burns, the insured is the winner. If it does not, the company wins. This is not so. The owner of the house always faces the risk of its destruction by fire. By the payment of a small fee he shifts the burden of this ever-present risk to the company. This transaction creates no

risks, but merely shifts the burden from the property owner
to the professional risk-bearer who is willing to assume it.

A wager, on the other hand, creates a risk. If one bets on
a horse race, there is no risk until he bets. Therefore, there
is no shifting of burden of risk in this latter situation, but
there is the creation of a new risk.

Insurance can be defined as the social device by which
individuals can transfer their chances of loss to a professional risk-bearing organization for a fee. Insurance substitutes for the uncertain cost of a possible loss the certain
small cost of protection against this loss.

The transfer of risks, however, involves more than merely
buying an insurance policy. To avoid any confusion between himself and the insurance company in case of loss,
the insurance-buyer must know the answers to these two
questions:

1. *What* risks have been transferred?

2. From what *property* have they been transferred?

The answer to the first question lies in the wording of the
insurance policy. The buyer should read it carefully, making
sure he understands not only what it covers, but what it does
not cover. If he bought the policy through a local insurance
agent or broker, he can get through that office a professional
explanation of any parts of the policy which may not be
quite clear to him.

The answer to the second question may not be as simple
as it appears. For example, a fire insurance policy may insure "dwelling and contents" at a given address. But unless the insurance-buyer has an astounding memory, that
word "contents" may trip him up if a fire destroys his home.
Because if that happens, he will have to prepare a list of
everything of value that was destroyed.

That can be difficult. Try it yourself. To make it a little easier, take just one room—let's say the living room. Without looking there, write down everything of value you can think of in that room. Then go through it and compare your list with what you find. You'll probably find at least one or two major things you'd completely forgotten.

The solution is to prepare an inventory. In the case of each article, the year it was purchased, its cost and its present value should be noted. A more elaborate inventory might include photographs of certain items. Again, professional help can be obtained from the local agent or broker who sold the policy.

An inventory is useless, however, unless it is (1) completely up to date and (2) available when needed. All new purchases should be noted immediately; also any values which may change with the passing of time. A copy of the inventory should be kept at the bank, or with the insurance agent or broker. If the only copy is kept at home, it may very well be destroyed by the same fire which destroys the possessions it records.

Most insurance companies have prepared inventory forms for the use of their policyholders. These inventories are available through local agents, and you may obtain yours from the agent who writes your household insurance. Typical pages from one of these inventories are shown immediately following. It will be seen that the inventory pages provide for the most common objects, and, in addition, blank spaces are available for listing any items not covered in the printed form.

Why

OU SHOULD MAKE AN INVENTORY

fter a fire it is practically imp
ble to remember everything

INVENTORY
of
PERSONAL PROPE
in the residence of

LIVING ROOM

ARTICLE	Date Purchased	ORIG CO
Rugs		
Carpets		
Chairs		
Tables		
Cabinets		
Couch		
Writing Desk		
Piano		
Musical Instruments		
Radio & TV Sets		
Clock		
Mirror		
Lamps		
Lighting Fixtures		
Drapes		
Curtains		
Window Shades		
Cushions		

DINING ROOM

No. Articles	ARTICLE	Date Purchased	ORIGINA COST
	Rugs		
	Carpets		
	Chairs		
	Tables		
	Buffet		
	China Cabinet		
	Clocks		
	Mirrors		
	Lamps		

KITCHEN, PANTRY & BREAKFAST ROOM

No. Articles	ARTICLE	Date Purchased	ORIGINAL COST	PRESEN VALUE
	Floor Covering			
	Chairs			
	Tables			
	Kitchen Cabinet			
	Refrigerator			
	Clock			

ARTICLE	Date Purchased
Rugs	
Carpets	
Chairs	
Tables	
Beds	
Mattresses	
Dressing Table	
Bureau	
Chest of Drawers	
Dresser	
Chaise Lounge	
Writing Desk	
Clocks	
Mirrors	
Lamps	
Lighting Fixtures	
Drapes	
Curtains	
Window Shade	
Prints	
Pictures (Pa	
Frames	
Toilet Arti	
Cedar Ch	
Bedding	
Clothin	
Radio	
Othe	

JEWELRY AND SILVERWAR

No. Articles	ARTICLE	Date Purchased	ORIGINAL COST

CLOTHING

No. Articles	ARTICLE	Date Purchased	ORIGINAL COST

22 GARAGE & OTHER BUILDINGS

No. Articles	ARTICLE	Date Purchased	ORIGINAL COST
	Automobiles		
	Auto Tools		
	Auto Accessories		
	Work Bench		
	Bicycles		
	Lawn Mowers		
	Garden Tools		
	Hoses		
	Porch Furniture		
	Other Property		
	Stored		

 **3,000 B.C.** CHINESE SHARED RISKS BY DISTRIBUTING THEIR CARGOES AMONG MANY BOATS BEFORE REACHING THE DANGEROUS YANGTZE RIVER RAPIDS

BABYLONIAN CODE OF KING HAMMURABI PROVIDED CRUDE FORM OF INSURANCE AGAINST THE PERILS OF TRAVELING 4,500 YEARS AGO **2,500 B.C.**

 **1,200 B.C.** FAMOUS HINDU DOCUMENT RECORDS IMPROVEMENTS IN CONTRACT OF PROTECTION DEVELOPED BY THE EARLIER BABYLONIANS

MERCHANTS OF ISLAND OF RHODES ESTABLISHED "RHODIAN SEA LAW" INCORPORATING BASIC IDEA OF CONTRIBUTIONSHIP IN INSURANCE **1,000 B.C.**

 **533 A.D.** ROMAN EMPEROR JUSTINIAN INCLUDED RHODIAN SEA LAW IN RECODIFICATION OF STATUTES DRAWN UP TO GOVERN FAR-FLUNG EMPIRE

3

Origin of Insurance Protection

The origin of property insurance is veiled in antiquity. Fragmentary records show that primitive systems for transferring chances of loss existed in Assyria nearly 4,500 years ago; in Babylon, in the twenty-third century before the Christian era; in India, more than 2,000 years ago; and among the Chaldeans and Chinese, many centuries ago.

The beginnings of insurance can be traced wherever men lived and traded under less primitive forms of civilization. As men became more civilized, they became more dependent upon one another and began to realize how many perils of loss they shared in common. Soon it became apparent that if they shared these losses, the cost to each man would be no more than the relatively small sum he contributed to the general fund out of which losses would be paid.

Marine insurance, which protects owners of ships and cargoes from losses due to the perils of the sea, was known in a primitive form in Greece as early as the third century A.D. Wealthy individuals provided a form of insurance known as bottomry by making loans to shipowners. If the ships and cargoes reached their destination safely, the money, plus interest, was returned to the lender. If a disaster occurred, the shipowner or merchant who had sought protection retained the money. Because stormy and pirate-infested seas held many perils for small boats in those days, money-lenders usually charged high rates of interest.

17

Chinese Application of Insurance Principles

The Chinese of many centuries ago are credited with the application of insurance principles. Early Chinese merchant shippers were troubled by the frequency with which their boats struck submerged rocks and sank with costly cargoes while going through the dangerous rapids of the Yangtze River. Since these boats and their cargoes represented the entire worldly possessions of their owners, such disasters often meant ruin for unfortunate shippers.

Finally the shippers worked out a clever system for spreading the chance of loss. They reasoned, for example, that if one hundred boats, each with one hundred packages, were stopped at the head of the rapids, each merchant could place one of his packages on each of the one hundred boats; then, if one or two boats were sunk, each merchant would lose only one or two packages, instead of one luckless merchant losing his entire shipment.

The same principle of "sharing the risk" underlies modern insurance; many property owners voluntarily assume the cost of a small contribution—the price they pay for protection—in order that no one of them may suffer a ruinous loss.

Histories of the Middle Ages bear numerous references to insurance in Iceland. England, Belgium, Italy, Russia, Portugal, Denmark, and Holland.

Lloyd's of London

Marine insurance developed rapidly, particularly in the great seafaring nation of Great Britain. Protection was furnished not by companies as we know them today but by bankers, merchants, and moneylenders, who engaged in insurance as a sideline to their regular occupations.

The most famous group of early marine insurers were the men who met at Lloyd's of London at the beginning of the eighteenth century. In those days Lloyd's was merely a coffee house in Tower Street and had no connection with in-surance. At one time or another there were in London many such gathering places, which served as convenient "clubs" for actors, authors, professional men and businessmen. Each coffee house attracted a particular type of following.

The men who frequented Lloyd's were the businessmen of the day—merchants, shippers, sea captains, and men interested in insurance. Since at Lloyd's one could obtain first news of ship arrivals, of impending voyages, and of disasters at sea, it was natural that businessmen who risked their money in providing protection for cargoes and ships should gather there.

From the methods of providing insurance at Lloyd's comes the origin of the word "underwriting," which is commonly used in the business today. When a shipowner desired insurance for his vessel, he would post a notice, naming the ship, its destination, the route to be followed, the amount of protection he wished, and any other pertinent information. Persons desiring to share in furnishing the required insurance coverage would then write under the name of the ship their names and the amount of risk they were willing to assume. Hence the term "underwriting," which, in insurance, has come to mean the use of sound judgment in determining whether to accept or to reject a risk.

Beginnings of Fire Insurance

The history of modern fire insurance dates from the great fire of London in September, 1666. Flames raged for five days, destroying practically the entire city. For more than 100 years thereafter the second day of September was set aside in London as a special memorial day.

The conflagration left thousands homeless. Thousands more became paupers. The devastation and hardship caused

1288 ENGLISH GUILD OF BLESSED MARY WITHHELD FIRE INSURANCE BENEFITS FROM PERSONS GUILTY OF "LUST, DICE-PLAYING, AND GLUTTONY"

EARLIEST KNOWN COMPLETE CONTRACT OF INSURANCE, COVERING VOYAGE OF SHIP "SANTA CLARA" WAS RECORDED AT PORT OF GENOA, ITALY

1347

1574 QUEEN ELIZABETH SIGNED BILL WHICH ESTABLISHED "CHAMBER OF INSURANCE" DESIGNED TO PROVIDE PROTECTION FACILITIES FOR SHIPPERS

LONDON'S FIRE LED DR. NICOLAS BARBON TO OPEN FIRST FIRE INSURANCE OFFICE IN HISTORIC VENTURE ONE YEAR LATER

1666

1680 COFFEE HOUSE OWNED BY EDWARD LLOYD BECAME A MEETING PLACE FOR SHIPPERS AND OTHERS WHO SOUGHT INSURANCE PROTECTION

by fire had never been more deeply impressed on the minds of the people. Out of this catastrophe came the first practical working of the idea of fire insurance.

The man who put the idea into reality was Dr. Nicolas Barbon, one of the colorful characters in English history. Dr. Barbon decided to establish the first office devoted entirely to fire insurance. His concern was a one-man enterprise that offered protection for owners of houses and buildings.

Although this pioneer lacked the financial strength and knowledge possessed by insurance companies today, he did prove that fire insurance could be provided successfully. In 1680 Barbon formed a partnership in order that he might divide the risks he had been assuming alone. Three years later saw the formation of a rival organization, the Friendly Society.

Barbon's office and the Friendly Society established practices that were followed by insurance companies for centuries to come. Both issued long-term policies and both maintained squads of "watermen" to help put out fires on property in which each company was interested.

The Hand in Hand Mutual Insurance Office, started in 1696, was the third fire insurance firm of note to be established in London. The original name of the office was "Contributors for Insuring Houses, Chambers or Rooms from Loss by Fire by Amicable Contribution within the cities of London and Westminster and the liberties thereof, and the places thereunto adjoining." The office soon adopted the shorter title, derived from the two clasped hands on the firm's emblem.

These three early insurance organizations were not companies in the sense of our modern corporations, owned by stockholders who purchase shares in the control and conduct of a business. They were either individual enterprises or partnerships and confined their insurance protection to buildings, mostly houses.

A revolutionary expansion of fire insurance protection was instituted in 1706 by Charles Povey, a London promoter of many varied enterprises and founder of the Exchange House Fire Office. Povey's contribution to the development of fire insurance was his willingness to furnish protection for goods and merchandise.

Hand in Hand   *Sun*

Early English fire marks were usually made of lead

The public was skeptical of Povey's project. Although he tried to extend the operations of his business throughout Great Britain and Ireland, he met with meager success. By 1710, Povey had organized another firm, the Sun Fire Office, which is in existence today and is regarded by many as the first modern fire insurance company. At first, however, it was not a corporation but a partnership limited to twenty-four members.

Granting of Royal Charters

The next milestone in the growth of property insurance protection was the granting of royal charters to British marine and fire insurance organizations. The first two chartered property insurance corporations were established in London in 1720. These companies, The London Assurance and The Royal Exchange Assurance, are in business today, operating on a world-wide basis.

Royal Exchange   London Assurance

Fire marks were placed on policyholders' buildings

Property insurance was now an established institution. No longer was protection against loss by fire and the perils of the sea made possible only by men who gave it their spare time, thought, and money. No longer were the vast majority of policies to be backed by the financial security of a single promoter, such as Dr. Nicolas Barbon or Charles Povey. The example set by The London Assurance and The Royal Exchange Assurance—sound protection backed by substantial funds—has been the pattern for leading companies formed since 1720.

1792 FIRST AMERICAN FIRE AND MARINE INSURANCE COMPANY WAS ORGANIZED IN ROOM WHERE DECLARATION OF INDEPENDENCE WAS SIGNED

FIRST INSURANCE AGENT WAS APPOINTED AT LEXINGTON, KENTUCKY, INAUGURATING PERSONAL SERVICE TO POLICYHOLDERS IN EVERY COMMUNITY

1807

1863 FIRST AMERICAN ACCIDENT POLICY WAS ISSUED DURING PERIOD WHEN RAILROADS WERE OPENING UP NEW FRONTIERS THROUGHOUT NATION

ANALYSIS OF BALTIMORE'S FIRE BY NATIONAL BOARD OF FIRE UNDERWRITERS LED TO PREVENTIVE INSPECTIONS OF ALL CITIES

1904

1943 COMPREHENSIVE INSURANCE EXAMINATIONS LED TO FIRST AWARDS OF THE PROFESSIONAL DESIGNATION "CHARTERED PROPERTY AND CASUALTY UNDERWRITER"

4

Development of Property Insurance
in the New World

It was only natural for merchants in the early days of American history to look to insurers in England for insurance against loss resulting from the destruction of their property by fire or other perils.

First evidence of an interest on the part of the colonists in developing their own insurance business is found in two historic publications. In 1721, Mr. John Copson of Philadelphia advertised in *The American Weekly Mercury* that he was about to open an "Office of Publick Insurance on Vessels, Goods and Merchandizes." There is no further record of Mr. Copson's venture.

Four years later, also in Philadelphia, there appeared a book by Francis Rawle, *Ways and Means for the Inhabitants of Delaware to Become Rich,* which classed insurance as "a worth-while branch of trade." The book was the first to be printed by Benjamin Franklin, who, twenty-seven years later, was to take part in forming one of the first insurance companies on the continent, The Philadelphia Contributionship.

The Friendly Society for the Mutual Insuring of Houses against Fire was organized under a royal charter in Charleston, South Carolina, in 1735. The Society remained in business only six years and little is known of its operations. Boston also boasted several early insurance offices.

Philadelphia, a leading commercial and cultural center of

the colonies, is often referred to as "the cradle of American fire insurance companies." Some of these Philadelphia insurance companies are the direct outgrowth of early volunteer fire-fighting organizations—predecessors of modern fire departments. By the middle of the eighteenth century there were in this city six such "fire brigades", including more than two hundred members.

Philadelphia contributionship   *Green Tree*

The Philadelphia Contributionship

In April, 1752, a number of the citizens who contributed to the support of these fire brigades organized The Philadelphia Contributionship for the Insurance of Houses from Loss by Fire. Like its namesake in London, this company soon became known as the "Hand in Hand" because of the emblem appearing on its fire mark and because many of the organizers had been members of the fire-fighting group of the same name. The company issued "perpetual" policies. Eligible property owners desiring protection "contributed" one large premium, which was then invested to produce sufficient interest income to pay losses suffered by policyholders. The Philadelphia Contributionship continues to operate on the same basis today. It confines its operations to limited amounts of liability on a few types of property located in and near the city in which it was founded.

After one serious loss, this pioneer company declined to provide insurance on houses surrounded by trees, contending that such obstructions made fire fighting difficult. In 1784, many contributors withdrew and formed a new company, The Mutual Assurance Company for Insuring Houses from Loss by Fire in and near Philadelphia. The Mutual Assurance did not hesitate to issue policies on buildings shaded by trees but charged an extra fee for such insurance. Widely known as the Green Tree Mutual, from the insignia used on its fire mark, this company also continues in business today.

Formation of Capital Stock Company in 1792

The forerunner of the kind of companies that provide most of the fire insurance in this country today was founded in Philadelphia in 1792. Like the two corporations formed in London in 1720, this company was a capital stock company— that is, its policies were backed by capital contributed by its stockholders.

Expansion of Insurance Companies

The development of both marine and fire insurance in this country followed closely the trend in England. The business of protection was gradually revised and strengthened as civilization in each country became more complex and business interests more far-flung. First there were enterprising merchants who agreed to risk part of their money in insurance on ships and cargoes. Next came the promoters who set up full-time insurance "offices" where policies could be written. The operation of such offices was backed by the financial integrity of a single individual or of a group of wealthy men. Then followed the organization of the mutual companies—the policyholders in many cases knowing each other intimately. Finally came the capital stock companies whose additional financial strength, in the form of capital funds plus growing reserves, permitted them to keep pace with the demands of a rapidly expanding nation.

As the young republic grew, Philadelphia shared its leadership with other cities—New York, Newark, Hartford, and Providence, to name only a few.

The early years of growth were not smooth sailing for some of the first American insurance companies. Disastrous fires frequently occurred, for cities and towns of that day were ill-equipped to meet serious fires. Companies with insufficient resources failed. Some property owners found their policies valueless. The stronger companies, however, survived these successive disasters, and learned by their own experiences that a conflagration provides the greatest test of sound fire insurance.

Test of Reliability of Early Insurance Companies

One of the early trials of the financial strength of property insurance companies in this country was the great New York fire of 1835. The citizens of New York who were "burned out" learned that the sounder companies, which had written insurance throughout the nation—the firms that had not put all their eggs in one basket—were able to pay their obligations in full. The example set by such companies continues to be followed to this very day.

The disastrous New York fire of December 15, 1835, began as a small fire, but a brisk wind whipping in from the northeast, fanned the flames and drove them on, destroying banks, importing houses, merchants' establishments, and offices of professional men. Only when a boundary had been created by the blasting of buildings was the fire checked.

It is difficult to conceive what this disaster meant to the New Yorkers of that day. Not only did it paralyze their business life, but it left them without a vision for the future. At one stroke the catastrophe wiped out all that had been accumulated in years of slow, painstaking effort.

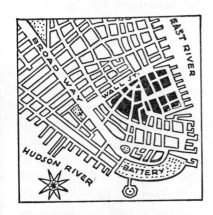

The fire of 1835 destroyed most of New York's business district

While New Yorkers were beginning to realize the full significance of the disaster, a mail coach was on its way, bearing word of the fire to insurance men in Hartford, Connecticut.

Ironically, the directors of one leading Hartford company were meeting on the evening of the New York fire and were forecasting the favorable future of the company. Its income had shown a healthy increase; its losses had been relatively small. A dividend for the stockholders, the first in seven years, was in sight. But the news they were about to receive was to cause them to face the crisis of their business lives.

When the president and the secretary of the company heard the report of the fire, they knew that the company's loss was heavy. However, they had no way of telling the full extent of their obligations. The detailed records upon which modern insurance companies maintain their liability had not yet been developed. There was nothing to do but face the situation as it unfolded.

The president went directly to one of the leading banks in the city and made arrangements to draw upon it without limit, pledging his personal resources as security for the good name of his company. With the secretary, he started out for New York.

Upon arrival in New York, the officers of that company set up a crude office on the outskirts of the charred area. Then they began the great task of paying claims. At first the rush was great. However, confidence increased and pressure eased as those who pressed forward talked with men who came away with their claims paid. Such scenes were typical of those repeated throughout the city as other responsible insurance companies marshalled every financial resource to see that each just claim was paid in full.

The New York fire of 1835 was, in many ways, a dramatic test of the strength and stability of the young American fire insurance business.

Property Insurance a Factor in Expansion of Nation

Property insurance was an important factor in making possible the rapid territorial and economic expansion of the United States during the nineteenth century. Establishment and development of new cities in frontier communities naturally required the services of insurance. Without some security from serious financial loss, many persons might have hesitated before setting up new homes and industries.

This rapid expansion meant that additional large sums of capital were necessary to provide the insurance protection required. To assist in providing this capital, foreign property insurance companies—most of them British—extended their operations in the United States. They transferred funds to this country and established separate United States branches to assume part of the burden of risk that had previously taxed American companies. The additional resources made available by these companies represented a substantial contribution to the capital necessary for adequate insurance protection during the period of the nation's greatest growth.

Many United States branches of British and other foreign companies continue to operate in this country today, conducting their affairs on the same basis as the American companies.

Property Insurance and the San Francisco Fire

With the advent of the twentieth century the United States had become one of the major powers in the family of nations. The fire insurance business had kept pace with this growth and had become one of the great financial institutions of the country. Within a few years, it faced one of the crucial tests in its history.

On April 18, 1906, 80,000,000 people of the United States received the tragic word that overnight thousands of their

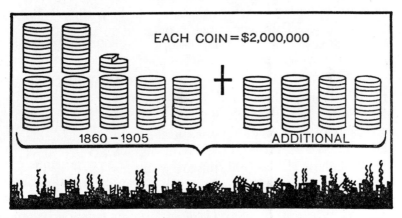

EACH COIN = $2,000,000

1860 – 1905   ADDITIONAL

Losses paid for San Francisco's fire of 1906 equalled all underwriting profits earned by insurance companies nationwide since 1860, plus $80,000,000

fellow citizens in San Francisco were homeless and that a proud American city had suffered the most serious property loss ever recorded—caused by an earthquake and resulting fire.

The fire insurance business received an impressive tribute, following the San Francisco tragedy, in the testimonial of the National Association of Credit Men. A committee from that association pointed out that many extraordinary conditions prevailed, that policies had been burned, that records had been lost. Yet, following a careful investigation, it was able to say:

> The people of San Francisco received their greatest aid in obtaining honest and liberal adjustments from honorable and fearless insurance companies which refused to be parties to agreements for arbitrary deductions and which paid their losses amounting to millions of dollars in a spirit of liberality and honesty.*

All told, $220,000,000 of fire insurance payments were made to the citizens of San Francisco to help them rebuild a greater city. This occurrence proved again the soundness of the fundamental principles upon which the property insurance business operates.

Another major test, although slower to develop, was provided by the national and world-wide depression of the nineteen-thirties. It was a period of financial disaster. Numerous banks, commercial institutions and manufacturing plants in every state failed. Millions were unemployed. Yet throughout this period, the fire insurance business maintained its stability and continued to pay claims for losses as they arose, thus permitting many businesses and homes to

---

* Bulletin of the National Association of Credit Men, Volume VIII, Number 7, New York, July 15, 1907.

survive. And it continued to demonstrate its belief in America's future by reinvesting millions of premium dollars in private enterprise and government credit.

Growth of Other Types of Insurance

During the nineteenth century, other branches of the insurance business joined property insurance in sharing many of the complex risks of modern living. The first attempts to sell life insurance to the public were made in Philadelphia in 1807 by Israel Whelen, an agent of the Pelican Life Insurance Company of London. No aggressive effort to sell life insurance was made for many years thereafter and the number of policies issued was small. The decade starting in 1843, however, saw the founding of fifteen companies, all of which are still among the nation's leading life insurance organizations and the progress has continued.

Note: In 1759, the Presbyterian Ministers' Fund was founded in Philadelphia. It is considered the first American corporation in the field of life insurance, although the company did not sell insurance to the general public.

Casualty Insurance

As business and life became more highly organized, the need for insurance protection grew in proportion. There was the need for protection against many new hazards and individuals and companies found themselves increasingly confronted with real and fancied claims.

Accident insurance was the first casualty coverage to be sold in America, a company being established for this purpose in 1864. This form of protection took great strides with each major development in transportation, since accident policies were frequently sold in connection with specific journeys.

Toward the end of the nineteenth century, health insurance was added as a rider to accident policies and later came to be sold either seperately or in combination. Around 1912 the first accident group policy was written, and today accident and health insurance written on a group or individual basis covers millions of people.

Liability insurance, protecting the policyholder against the claims of "third parties," was instituted in 1885 with the marketing of employer's liability policies. Other forms of liability insurance soon followed in rapid succession. The advent of the automobile and automobile liability policies, around the turn of the century, has resulted in bringing the volume of liability insurance to increasingly higher levels.

Since the passage of workmen's compensation laws beginning in the first part of the century, workmen's compensation insurance has almost entirely replaced employer's liability insurance. Under this type of insurance, compensation benefits, including medical and hospital expenses, are paid by the insurance company or self-insured employer. Compensation is payable only for injuries, disease and death sustained by a workman while in "the course of employment." In recent years some states have enacted "disability benefits laws," thus providing compensation benefits because of "off-job" sickness or injury.

Enlightened employers and insurance companies together have cooperated in safeguarding dangerous machines and processes and in safety education of employees. This, plus greater care on the part of employees themselves, has brought remarkable improvements to industrial safety records.

For those engaged in business and manufacturing, other types of coverages were developed. The large volume of energy that is pent up in boilers can cause terrific damage if it is suddenly released when the boiler bursts. Originally started as an engineering inspection service, a function still very important today, one company began to issue insurance policies on boilers in 1866. At the present time, boiler and machinery insurance can be written to cover indirect as well as direct losses.

Protection against theft is one of the age-old problems of mankind. Although earlier attempts had been made, the first successful underwriting of burglary and theft policies dates from 1892.

Business concerns have also found it necessary to protect their interests against theft and embezzlement on the part of their own employees. Many employees of banks and business organizations daily handle hundreds or even thousands of dollars of other people's money. This has led to the increased use of fidelity bonding under which an insurance company makes good to the employer or other policyholder the amount of theft or other loss. Fidelity bonds were originally sold in 1876.

Surety bonding followed closely after fidelity bonding. These bonds indemnify for loss to others where someone such as a building contractor fails to carry out the obligations to which he is committed.

Special groups of companies handle various phases of aviation insurance. The modern passenger airplane not only faces the perils of millions of dollars of damage to the ship and its cargo in the event of a crash or a fire, but there are large amounts of liability involved for possible death and injury claims.

Each branch of the business is a major institution in its own right. Each contributes to the security and peace of mind of millions of persons who have a financial interest in losses that might be caused by death, injury, ill health, the destruction of property or the harmful actions of others.

5

Major Types of
Insurance Organizations

The average property owner transfers to a professional risk-bearer—an insurance company—the risk of destruction of his property as a result of fire or other similar causes. Let us, therefore, consider briefly the major types of property insurance organizations serving the American public today.

Before a company can be established, its organizers must obtain a charter from the state in which the company will be incorporated. State laws relating to corporations and to insurance companies require that the new company meet certain financial and legal standards before actual operations can begin. Once in operation, the company is subject to the continuous supervision of public officials in each state in which it does business.

The first insurance companies, both here and in England, were mutual organizations. Numerically, the great majority of mutual companies were, and continue to be, local organizations, each writing business only in a limited area.

In a young nation in which rural neighbors recognized the value of cooperation in such activities as planting and harvesting, the formation of small township or county mutual insurance companies was a logical development. When a farmer's property was destroyed by fire, his neighbors frequently donated their time to help rebuild it. Soon farmers realized they could put this cooperation on a more business-like basis by banding together to establish small insurance companies whose assets consisted solely of the premium payments each farmer contributed. The farmer became part owner of the company, as well as a policyholder. He shared the responsibilities of the business as well as its earnings.

The organizers of these small mutual companies did not set up a capital fund. Instead, all policyholders agreed to contribute extra funds in the event the losses sustained made such action necessary. This right to assess policyholders for additional funds is a characteristic of the mutual plan of organization. Another characteristic is a refund in the form of "dividends" at the end of the policy year, if premiums are more than ample to meet losses and expenses.

As our national economy expanded and became more complex, some mutual companies broadened the scope of their operations to keep pace with this growth. These larger mutual companies operate on a nationwide basis. They charge a fixed premium in advance, with the understanding that the right to assess policyholders will be limited or eliminated entirely. In place of the right of assessment, these companies substitute the accumulation of surplus funds. These funds represent a portion of the company's earnings which, instead of being paid to policyholders, is set aside for development and for meeting unusual losses or other contingencies in the future.

Capital Stock Companies

With the growth of industry and the insurance requirements of the nation, the need for a substantial reserve fund to guarantee the payment of losses became apparent. Businessmen and even individual owners of small homes required full insurance protection with no risk of additional assessment. This spurred the development of capital stock insurance companies, so called because their organizers provide capital and reserves by the purchase of stock. In addition, the stockholders, who share ownership of these companies, also subscribe a surplus fund, usually at least equal to the capital fund.

Today, state laws require substantial capital and reserves for any company going into the business of fire insurance.

In addition to the capital and initial surplus paid in by stockholders, such companies generally allocate to their surplus fund a substantial share of the earnings that have been accumulated. This money can serve as an additional protection for policyholders. This plan follows the practice of prudent businessmen in all lines of endeavor to plow back a part of their earnings to provide extra funds for growth and to meet unpredictable emergencies.

Shares of capital stock insurance companies are available through established investment channels. Such securities are widely distributed and are held by individuals, colleges, foundations and other groups whose chief concern is stability. The insurance companies themselves have large reserves represented in their investment portfolios. They serve a valuable function in the country's economic life by providing a stable investment market for government, state and municipal bonds and the seasoned securities of industry.

Capital stock companies generally sell their policies to the public only through local agents and brokers, independent businessmen whose sole compensation is the commissions on the policies they sell. A few, called "direct writers," sell direct to the public through salaried employees.

Most of the large fire insurance companies in the country are capital stock companies. They provide the stability and security that are essential not only for the large business organization with heavy requirements for insurance but for the small insured as well.

Reciprocal Exchanges

Reciprocal exchanges, often referred to as "insurance companies," are not companies in the same sense of the word as are either capital stock or mutual organizations. In contrast, a reciprocal exchange is not a corporation.

Under the reciprocal insurance plan, the policyholders, who are known as subscribers, agree to exchange insurance with each other. Each policyholder individually assumes his proportionate share of every other policyholder's risk. In return, he accepts the individual promises of other policyholders that each will pay a stipulated proportion of his loss if one should occur. These promises are not collective. No policyholder can be held liable for more than his proportion of any loss—even if some of the other policyholders fail to meet their obligations.

To illustrate the liability, or responsibility, of each subscriber in a reciprocal exchange, let us consider a sample case. Assume that a reciprocal exchange has five subscribers, each subscriber seeking $10,000 of insurance on like properties.

If subscriber A had a total loss, he would ordinarily collect $2,500 from each of the other four. But if one of the other subscribers, subscriber B, for example, was unable to pay, that fact would not affect the contributions of subscribers C, D, or E. These three would contribute only $2,500 each. Subscriber A would then be the loser to the extent of B's default.

On the other hand, subscriber A is not liable himself for more than $2,500 in case of the total destruction of any one of the four properties. However, should all four of the other properties be destroyed, he would of course have to pay $10,000.

Thus it can be seen that each subscriber who has placed a risk of $10,000 with the exchange has transferred the risk on his own property to four other subscribers. In consideration of their agreement to "protect" him to the extent of $10,000 in event of loss, he, in turn, has assumed a risk amounting to $2,500 on each of the four other subscribers. Each subscriber thus assumes a total risk of $10,000. While a capital stock or mutual company's funds may be used in its entirety to meet claims against the company, the funds held by a reciprocal exchange for the account of its individual subscribers cannot be so used because the subscribers have assumed no joint obligations. They operate as individuals, using a common office for the conduct of their affairs, and employ the services of a common manager, usually known as an "attorney in fact."

Types of Lloyd's Organizations

There are two types of Lloyd's organizations doing business in this country: brokers who do business through Lloyd's of London and firms whose operations are patterned after Lloyd's.

Lloyd's of London is not an insurance company. It is a market place where insurance protection may be purchased, just as a stock exchange is a market place for the purchase of stocks. Insurance is placed with individual underwriters or groups of underwriters who are "members at Lloyd's." These underwriters accept all or a portion of a risk that may be offered, and each member assumes personal liability for the amount of risk he accepts.

Self-Insurance

In a few instances, governmental bodies or owners of a large number of properties have set up so-called "self-insurance" funds as a substitute for protection purchased from an insurance company. While efforts are made to provide capital for these "self-insurance" funds, few of them conform

to insurance principles or utilize proper inspection and prevention methods, and a number of such plans have failed
spectacularly. The phrase "self-insurance" is a contradiction
in terms. In these instances, the risk is assumed rather than
transferred to a professional risk-bearer.

Michigan began a self-insurance fund in 1913, originally
requiring the various governmental divisions to pay in premiums. By February 1951, there was $1,750,000 in the fund.
That month the State Office Building burned with a loss of
$5,271,000. A year later a riot and fire occurred at Jackson
State Prison with a loss of $1,483,970. Clearly, the insurance
fund was inadequate to cover the loss, and the taxpayers of
the state were forced to make up the difference.

Colorado set up an insurance fund in 1926. The following
year it faced a loss of $86,000 at the State Agricultural Col-
lege with less than half that amount in the fund. In 1930, a
$250,000 loss took place at the State Penitentiary in Canon
City. A few years later the legislature abolished the state
fund and passed a bill which permits the purchase of fire
insurance through private insurance companies on state
buildings and institutions.

These are but two examples of many which illustrate the
fallacy of an actuarially unsound self-insurance program.
Professional risk bearers have the financial stability and
spread of risk which is so essentially a part of insurance company underwriting.

6

The Insurance Contract

The tangible evidence of the transfer of a risk to an insurance company is the insurance policy. This policy is a contract setting forth the scope of the protection given to the property owner.

To grasp the fundamentals of a property insurance contract, consider the basic elements of a typical fire insurance policy,* used in this country. When insurance was in its infancy, it was customary for each company to make up its own contract of protection. Policies issued by different companies varied widely in their provisions and in the degree of protection afforded. Such variations led to embarrassment for property owners who frequently held several differently worded contracts covering a single piece of property, and these differences often caused confusion in the settling of amounts due in case of a fire loss.

With the turn of the century, a uniform standard policy came into use in the great majority of states.

Only risks that might involve a property owner in a dollar-and-cents loss can be transferred to an insurance company. Values based on personal sentiment alone cannot be insured. A property owner can purchase insurance against financial loss caused by a fire that might destroy his house. But a bundle of old love letters, no matter how highly they may be prized from a sentimental viewpoint, would have no insurable value.

---

* See the New York Standard Fire Insurance Policy, 1943, which is in use in a majority of states, Appendix D, page 114.

Meaning of "Insurable Interest"

It may help our understanding if we remember that it is incorrect to speak of "insuring a piece of property." Actually, the insurance company insures the owner against loss to his property. The person or persons to whom an insurance policy is issued must be the ones who would suffer monetary loss if the property described in the policy were destroyed. They must have, to quote a technical phrase, "an insurable interest" in the property. This rule is important. If people were permitted to buy insurance on property whose destruction would result in no financial loss to them, any payment made after a fire would be in the nature of a gambling gain. The sole purpose of fire insurance is to indemnify property owners for their actual losses.

Policy Provisions

The basic fire insurance policy insures a property owner against direct loss by fire and lightning.*

Because policies are not identical in every state, it is possible to comment on policy provisions only in general terms. Basically, these provisions can be viewed from two chief points:

1. The provisions that explain the risks covered and the risks excluded.

2. The provisions that should be considered before a loss occurs and those that should be considered after a fire.

Risks not covered in such a fire policy include losses caused by invasion, insurrection, riot, civil war, civil commotion, and theft. The property owner must also "use all reasonable means to save and preserve the property" at the time of a fire or when the property is endangered by a near-by fire.

---

* See Essential Coverages, page 60.

For example, furniture carried from a burning building should not be left exposed to the weather. However, the property owner is not expected to risk his personal safety to safeguard such property.

A few specific items—for example, money; securities, and evidences of debt—are not covered under the fire policy.

Losses caused by war are excluded from the protection promised under the policy. The degree of risk of war is not predictable. An insurance company has a fundamental obligation to its policyholders to preserve its financial stability so as to be able to pay normal losses when they occur. This integrity might be seriously threatened if the company suffered unexpected war losses of catastrophic proportions.

Among the provisions to be considered is a clause in the standard fire insurance contract stating that the policy shall be void if the property owner has wilfully concealed or misrepresented any material fact.

For example, concealment has been defined as designed and intentional withholding of any fact material to the risk, which the insured ought in honesty and good faith to communicate.

Fire insurance policies, which are most commonly written for one, three, or five years, generally take effect at noon, standard time at the place where the property is located, on the date agreed upon by the agent and the insured. Coverage runs to noon of the specified expiration date.

Sometimes policies do not run their full term. They may be cancelled by either the company or the insured. Immediate cancellation may be effected when the insured himself takes the initiative. If the company wishes to cancel, it usually must give the insured written notice five days (in some states, ten days) before the insurance is to be terminated. This gives the property owner time to seek protection from some other company.

After the Loss

After a fire has caused a loss covered under the policy, the contract provides that the insured, the property owner, shall:

1. Give written notice to the company. Customarily, written or verbal notice to the insurance agent will suffice.
2. Protect the property from further damage.
3. Submit, within a specified period after the fire, a proof-of-loss, signed and sworn to by the insured.
4. Make available to the company as often as may be reasonably required, all books of account, bills, invoices and other vouchers and shall permit copies thereof to be made.

On rare occasions the company and the policyholder fail to agree on the amount of a loss. The policy provides for such a possibility in its "Appraisal" section. The procedure is for the property owner and the company each to select a competent and disinterested appraiser. The two appraisers select an umpire. If they fail to select an umpire after a certain period of time, the property owner or the company may appeal to a court of record to appoint one.

When the appraisers disagree in establishing the value and the amount of loss involving the property destroyed by fire, their differences shall be submitted to the umpire. An award in writing by any two shall determine the amount of actual cash value and loss. This section is interesting for the logical steps it establishes to make certain that the property owner shall get the fairest possible settlement. It is seldom used, however, since only a few of the hundreds of thousands of losses occurring yearly go to appraisal.

Through its early provision for such procedure, the property insurance business was one of the pioneers in introducing the modern principle of arbitration in business relation-ships, and this principle has been adopted by progressive leaders in many other fields.

1. REPORT LOSS

2. SAFEGUARD REMAIN-ING PROPERTY

3. PREPARE INVENTORY

4. SUBMIT "PROOF OF LOSS"

What to do after a loss

Replacement of Property

There are other clauses of the policy that also refer to conditions applying after a loss. For example, the company reserves the right to replace property lost in a fire instead of paying the loss in cash. This clause is rarely applied in a settlement, however. It serves merely to emphasize the primary purpose of insurance—that of furnishing indemnity, not of creating a profit.

If two or more companies have identical policies covering the same property, in case of loss each pays its proportion of the policyholder's claim. To illustrate, if the property owner carries $3,000 of fire insurance in Company A and $2,000 in Company B, he will receive in the event of a $1,000 loss, 60 per cent of the loss ($600) from Company A and 40 per cent ($400) from Company B.

A loss is payable, as a rule, sixty days after the property owner's sworn statement, called the "proof-of-loss", is received by the company. Companies take pride in the fact that they pay claims much earlier than the sixty-day limit. This leeway merely gives them time to study all details of a loss if the proof-of-loss is particularly complicated or if further investigation seems desirable. The vast majority of losses are concluded through complete cooperation between the adjuster and the insured, the former assisting the latter in the final preparation of the proof-of-loss.

Protecting the Interest of the Mortgagee

In cases where the property involved has been mortgaged, the lender has a vital interest in seeing that proper insurance protection is in force at all times. If the property should be destroyed by fire or other perils the security for the loan would be impaired. These mortgage interests are recognized in a special clause in the policy, or in an endorsement, outlining the relationship of the company, the property owner, and the mortgagee.

The insured should read his contract and familiarize himself with its provisions. Most people fail to do so. But even when such confidence in the companies exists on the part of the policyholder, the latter may not understand exactly what he bought. To minimize the possibility of misunderstanding, just as in a real estate transaction, the insured should read his contract carefully and, if necessary, have it explained to him by a competent insurance agent or broker.

The Coinsurance Clause

The property owner should not only be familiar with the provisions of the property insurance contract he intends to purchase, he should also understand his protection requirements fully in order to be able to answer intelligently the question: "How much coverage shall I buy?" If his property is located in a community having adequate fire protection, he knows that most fires are extinguished before the property is totally destroyed. He may, therefore, be tempted to buy only enough insurance to cover his loss in the event of partial destruction, and to take a chance on the more remote possibility that a fire might totally destroy the property. The more prudent will buy sufficient to protect them in the event of a total loss, realizing that such a loss would be far more disastrous to their finances than would only partial destruction.

The probability of a partial loss on property protected by an efficient fire department is obviously much greater than the probability of a total loss. It is also true that a very small loss is more probable than a loss involving even a moderate percentage of the property's value. As the amount of insurance approximates the total value of the property, the probability of a company's having a loss to the full amount of its policy decreases. Thus it would seem that the property owner who carried full insurance would be contributing an unduly large share to the funds out of which all losses would be paid. Consider this example: Jones and Smith each own buildings valued at $10,000. Jones, gambling on the fact that most fires result in partial losses, purchases only $2,000 of fire insurance. Smith, the more prudent property owner, carries $8,000 of coverage. If both men call on their insurance company to reimburse them in the event of $2,000 fire losses each, Jones, the property owner who gambled, will in effect be seeking the same indemnity as Smith although he has paid only one-quarter of the premium paid by the more prudent insured.

In fairness to all policyholders, insurance companies have adopted the practice of charging a lower rate when the

TWO EXAMPLES OF COINSURANCE IN OPERATION

A

80% CLAUSE AT REDUCED RATE

PREMIUM $10.00 ANNUALLY

B

PREMIUM $5.00 ANNUALLY

FULL PROTECTION RE-QUIRED: 80% OF VALUE

HALF OF REQUIRED PROTECTION: 40%

HALF OF PROPERTY BURNS

HALF OF PROPERTY BURNS

LOSS PAYMENT: 100%

LOSS PAYMENT: 50%

property owner accepts a condition in his policy requiring him to carry insurance for an amount representing a substantial proportion of the property's value. The amount of insurance required under this condition is not specified in dollars and cents. Instead, the clause requires that insurance shall be carried for a stated percentage of the value of the property. The most frequent requirement is 80 per cent.

With each increase in the percentage, a reduction in the rate charged is usually granted. This condition in the contract is variously known as the coinsurance clause or the reduced rate contribution or average clause.

This coinsurance or reduced rate clause is offered on business and commercial properties. It is seldom used on properties covering private dwellings.

In actual practice the operation of the coinsurance clause is simple. Let us assume that a property owner owns a building worth $10,000. He elects to purchase insurance subject to an 80 per cent coinsurance clause. This would require him to carry at least $8,000 of insurance. If he complies with that requirement, he will collect an amount sufficient to cover any loss up to $8,000, the amount of the insurance purchased. He is permitted to carry more insurance than the $8,000 required if he wishes to do so. If he should elect to carry $10,000 insurance, he would collect for any loss up to $10,000.

If, on the other hand, having elected to carry his insurance subject to an 80 percent coinsurance clause he actually carries only $4,000 insurance, he would recover only 50 per cent of any loss not to exceed, of course, the face value of his policy, because he carried only 50 per cent of the insurance required under the terms of his policy.

In brief, by having this clause in the policy, the property owner simply agrees to keep himself insured up to a specified percentage of the value of the property, for example, 80 per cent. If he maintains insurance up to 80 per cent, the loss will be paid just as if there were no coinsurance clause. If he insured for only 70 per cent, he would get seven-eighths of the amount of the loss. If he insured for only 60 per cent, he would get six-eighths of the amount of the loss.

Some people believe that in the event of any loss, either partial or total, the property owner is entitled to collect only that percentage of his loss which is stated in the coinsurance clause. For example, they think that if a man owns a building worth $10,000 and carries $8,000 of insurance with an 80 per cent coinsurance clause, he will collect only 80 per cent of any loss. Thus, if he has a $1,000 loss, they believe he would collect only $800.

This impression is incorrect. On the contrary, a property owner who purchases insurance subject to the conditions of a coinsurance clause suffers no penalty whatever in the settlement of any loss, provided he carries an amount of insurance equal to or in excess of the percentage of the value of the property required in the clause. In fact, the property owner benefits through the reduced rate he receives when he purchases a policy with a coinsurance clause.

The fire insurance contract is the product of many years of gradual evolution. In its development the property insurance business has striven for more than two centuries to meet the changing protection needs of the public and to assure equitable treatment among all policyholders.

7

Some Basic Insurance Principles

In the successful operation of present-day insurance companies, certain principles have evolved which are followed generally by most fire insurance companies:

Similar Risks—Each company seeks to insure a large number of similar properties in different locations. By similar is meant properties that face about the same risk of being destroyed by fire and are roughly comparable in size and value. While various properties in the same community may be entirely different, an insurance company will try to get a large number of each "class" of risk (private dwelling, retail store, or manufacturing plant) on its books from communities over the country or some other large area. By such diversification and limitation of risk the insurance company seeks to lessen its chances of a very large or disproportionate loss.

Limitation of Risk—Prudent insurance companies will not retain an excessive amount of liability in one area. They will either decline the business or reinsure part or all of the risk with another company.

Loss Prevention—Insurance companies send their loss prevention engineers to large commercial and business properties to advise policyholders how to avoid or reduce the number of fires or accidents. Sometimes insurance engineers are invited to consult with a policyholder's architect before the property is built to suggest the best ways to guard against fire and accidents and to incorporate these ideas in the plans for the building. The policyholder has the further incentive of knowing that the cost of his insurance is reduced if he can reduce his likelihood of losses.

Inspection Service—Insurance inspectors visit large properties periodically not only to make a detailed survey but also to help the policyholder maintain established good practices of fire and accident prevention. The insurance inspector is an important aid to the policyholder in cutting losses and insurance costs.

In addition, insurance companies conduct a year-'round campaign for safety and accident and fire prevention in the schools, colleges and with the public. Efforts to teach the principles of fire safety and safe driving practices in the high schools are encouraged country-wide by the insurance business.

Reserves—Down through history, insurance has faced the recurring crisis of conflagration or other events causing sudden huge insured losses. Company resources are the basis for large reserves to meet these catastrophes. In recent decades, state laws have required ample reserves for any company doing an insurance business in the state. Today, insurance reserves are stronger than at any time in the past. Not a single company suspended or limited payments following the great Northeast Storm of November 1950 despite the fact that the total number of claims was greater than for any disaster in history and, for a number of companies, the effects of the storm meant doubling the number of claims handled in a single year. The stock companies also successfully weathered the more than 1,000,000 claims totalling in excess of $200,000,000 that resulted from Hurricanes Carol, Edna and Hazel in 1954.

8

Role of Local Insurance Representatives

In the average community the business of most insurance companies is handled by local insurance agents. Most insurance agents operate as independent businessmen. Their training and experience qualify them for appointment by one or more insurance companies to represent the companies in their communities.

In larger cities property insurance is frequently sold also through brokers. The chief difference between an agent and a broker is that the broker is not under contract to represent any particular companies and theoretically acts as the property owners' representative.

In actual practice responsible agents and brokers both represent their policyholders' interests equally well. Both analyze the hazards that threaten financial loss to property owners. Just as lawyers diagnose the problems of their clients and advise them on legal procedure, local agents and brokers study the protection needs of their clients and prescribe insurance to fit those requirements. Over 200,000 agents and brokers are active today, serving property owners in communities ranging from the largest cities to the smallest hamlets throughout the United States.

"Insurance service" is no idle phrase. Agents and brokers throughout the country are providing insurance protection needed by the individual or by the largest corporation. If a local insurance man is to render helpful service, he must be familiar with all of the various types of contracts. He must also have a background of practical experience that will enable him to fit the various coverages to property owners' needs. In every state, local agents must qualify for special licenses issued by the State Insurance Department. In many states, success in a written examination is a necessary qualification.

When a property owner buys insurance, he receives a policy, the written contract issued by the company that has agreed to assume his risk. The property owner when he transfers a risk is obviously buying not only a policy but a complete insurance service, including the expert help of the local agent and the promise of protection of the company issuing the policy.

Some Functions of the Agent

After the customer's fire insurance needs have been determined the agent proceeds to "write the policy." This requires filling out certain necessary information on the policy. The amount of insurance purchased, the cost, the name of the person insured, the term of the contract and a brief description of the property must be shown on the policy or on special forms to be attached to the policy. Two extra copies of this basic information are made.

The agent sends one of these copies, called the "daily report," to the company, retaining the other for his own files. The policy itself goes to the insured with a suggestion that it be read carefully and kept in a safe place.

The job of the insurance agent or broker is far from complete when he delivers the policy and collects the premium. Because the promise of protection runs for a specified length of time, the agent takes pride in rendering continuous service to property owners during the life of the policy. Since

1. TECHNICAL ADVISOR WITH PROFESSIONAL RESPONSIBILITIES

2. SURVEYS CLIENT'S INSURANCE NEEDS

3. PREPARES POLICY — SENDS COPY TO COMPANY

4. TAILORS PROTECTION TO CHANGING NEEDS

5. AIDS CLIENT IN LOSS PREVENTION

6. PROVIDES TECHNICAL ADVICE AT TIME OF LOSS

Continuing services of an insurance agent

property insurance policies are generally sold for periods of one, three, or five years, much may happen while the policy remains in force. By keeping in constant touch with the property owner, the insurance agent renders valuable service in fitting insurance programs to changing needs and requirements.

The insurance agent, using the facilities of the companies he represents, serves his clients in another important manner —that is, in preventing losses. For example, by recommending the segregation of hazardous materials, or the installation of automatic sprinkler equipment and fire doors and extinguishers, an agent can often help to reduce many fire hazards. The reduction or elimination of major fire hazards may make property eligible for lower insurance rates.

When a loss occurs, the local insurance agent is immediately available. He is the one who secures all necessary information from the insured. He prepares a notice of loss form and sends it on to the company. Arrangements are then immediately made for the appointment of an adjuster.

Finally, the local knowledge of the agent is important in helping to prevent the saddling of the excessive losses of the few on the many. For example, if the agent avoids the issuing of policies to the property owner with a long record of suspicious fires, he benefits the entire community since payment of losses caused by dishonest persons would automatically increase the cost of fire insurance for all.

9

Scope of Property Insurance Protection

The scope of protection available to property owners is immeasurably greater today than it was a generation ago. As commerce, industry and personal affairs have become more complex, the insurance business has kept pace by creating new safeguards against financial loss. Literally hundreds of individual types of property insurance contracts are at the disposal of the homeowner or businessman who seeks fullest protection for the financial investment represented by his property. Against practically every peril to which property is exposed there is today some form of property insurance coverage.

Subjects of Protection

Not all property is exposed to identical perils. Thus a property owner does not have to use all of the available insurance policies in his search for adequate coverage.

The loss of a ring by fire or theft may inconvenience an individual but will not seriously affect his ability to carry on his daily affairs. The loss of other types of property, on the other hand, may produce disastrous results. To illustrate, the destruction of a person's home or place of business by fire, windstorm, or other peril would be ruinous.

Thus, insurance coverage can be grouped into two general classifications:

1. Coverages that are essential because, lacking insurance, destruction of the property by any peril would result in a catastrophic loss to the owner.
2. Coverages that are desirable for maximum protection but which are not absolutely necessary because, without insurance, the loss of the property would not be disastrous to the owner.

The differing requirements of each property owner represent a challenge that can be met only through intelligent appraisal of his individual needs. In this connection, local insurance agents and brokers render valuable service in helping property owners analyze their requirements so that:

1. All essential coverages are provided.
2. The purposes and functions of all desirable coverages are fully appreciated.

Essential Coverages

Let us consider the problems of a typical homeowner seeking adequate property insurance protection.

Fire and lightning insurance is an essential coverage in virtually every program anywhere because fire is a peril that may, at any time, produce a crippling financial loss.

Windstorms, cyclones, tornadoes, hurricanes, hailstorms and explosions are also possible threats to his security.

Insurance against such perils is essential to all property owners everywhere, because they are common to everyone and any one of them may cause a loss just as disastrous as one caused by fire. If the likelihood of such a loss seems remote, the rate charged for insurance will be low enough to justify its purchase. It should be borne in mind that while fires may be prevented through caution or limited in extent through effective fire fighting, insurance represents the only protection available to property owners against loss due to these natural elements. The best fire department is helpless in minimizing the fury of a tornado or hurricane.

Insurance against windstorm, hail, explosion, riot, riot attending a strike, civil commotion, aircraft, vehicles, and smoke may be purchased in a single endorsement, attached to a fire policy, known as the Extended Coverage Endorsement. The chance that property may be totally destroyed

Extended coverage endorsement protects against loss from all these perils

by falling aircraft is no longer considered fanciful. The explosion of gas appliances or a gas main in the street may be equally destructive.

A number of other perils that confront the homeowner— accidental discharge, leakage or overflow of water or steam; sudden and accidental tearing asunder, cracking, burning or bulging of a steam or hot water heating or storage system; vandalism and malicious mischief; vehicles owned or operated by the insured or by a tenant of the described premises; fall of trees; objects falling from the weight of ice, snow or sleet; freezing of plumbing, heating and air conditioning systems and domestic appliances; collapse of building(s); landslide; breakage of glass—have been put together in the Additional Extended Coverage Endorsement. Under certain circumstances, any of them could produce a severe loss. This endorsement is available to policyholders with fire insurance and extended coverage in most areas. In addition even broader forms are available such as the so-called dwelling building(s) special form, dwelling building(s) and contents-broad form, comprehensive dwelling policy and homeowners policy forms. New insurance forms are constantly being developed as the need for new types of protection becomes apparent.

Other Essential Coverages

The average home owner possesses a number of articles, such as jewelry or furs, having relatively high values. These articles may be subject to loss by certain perils to which the home itself is not exposed. For example, they may be lost or stolen outside the home. A broad form of coverage for such property is known as the inland marine floater, a direct descendant of ocean marine insurance, which was developed early in the history of the business to provide protection against a variety of perils and which follows property wherever it may go. Today, inland marine insurance protects property owners against all risks subject to a relatively few exceptions.

Since the purpose of this chapter is to acquaint the reader with the variety and scope of property insurance available to the homeowner, an analysis of the many coverages available for industry and business will not be discussed.

Inland marine insurance approaches all-risk protection

Brief mention should be made of the numerous types of
insurance issued by casualty insurance companies, among
which are those designed to protect an individual against
loss resulting from his legal responsibilities.   For example,
the owner or driver of an automobile may be held legally
liable for the death of a person in an accident.   Insurance to
protect that liability is essential.   The man carrying an um-
brella in a crowd may be held liable for gouging the eye of

Casualty insurance provides protection against perils like these

another person. Insurance protecting him against such loss is essential. The homeowner may be held liable for injury to the milkman if he slips on Junior's roller skates, which have been left on the back stoop. All these contingencies, and many others, may be covered by various forms of casualty insurance.

Various coverages may be combined in multiple line "package forms" and policies are provided that give the householder the combined protection of fire, theft, liability and casualty insurance.

Property is seldom destroyed without consequential losses. For example, homes are built to be lived in. If a home should be destroyed, the owner would be obliged to live elsewhere while his home is being rebuilt. The rent that he would pay during this period would represent a loss as actual as the destruction of the home itself. It would be logical, therefore, to insure against such a loss through the purchase of rental value insurance.

If business property is destroyed, a similar type of coverage is available. Businesses are conducted for the income they produce; thus if the property is destroyed, the income is also destroyed. Insurance for the protection against loss of that income is known as business interruption insurance or use and occupancy insurance.

Each type of property insurance available today was developed to fill a specific need caused by the existence of a specific peril. Some coverages that may seem highly essential to one property owner may be desirable but not absolutely necessary to his neighbor. For maximum security, each property owner should cooperate with a qualified insurance agent or broker in analyzing the perils to which his property is exposed and the insurance coverages that will furnish necessary safeguards against financial loss.

10

Operation of a Property Insurance Company

What happens in an insurance company office to produce dependable protection against so many chances of serious loss?

When a local insurance agent writes a fire policy, he prepares two copies of a special report—known as a daily report—listing basic information regarding the risk. He sends one copy of this information to the company, retaining the other copy for his records. The company's copy is the sole tangible evidence that the company has of the insurance transaction. En route from the local agent to the company, the report passes through a stamping or audit bureau, usually at the Rating Bureau, where the data relative to the insurance is checked to assure proper rate of premium and form of coverage.

Since no company, for its own protection and that of its policyholders, would knowingly accept a risk covering property owned by a person with an unsatisfactory record the name of the policyholder is checked against a comprehensive file. Occasionally the company will procure detailed information about the property owner from organizations specializing in investigating the character, general habits, and credit standing of individuals and business organizations.

Once it is established that the purchaser of insurance is a desirable risk the daily report goes to a "map clerk." Here begins one of the most interesting operations in the entire handling of the report. Many insurance companies maintain a set of maps showing in detail the location and type of construction of every building and the fire protection facilities in approximately 12,000 cities and towns in the country. A person who lives in any but the smallest community could walk into such an insurance company's head office and identify on the appropriate map a small-scaled reproduction of the building in which he lives, the shops in which he makes his purchases, and practically every other structure in town.

When the map clerk gets the daily report, he locates the property involved and pencils on the company's map the policy number, the amount and type of insurance, and the expiration date of the policy. While formerly all risks, both large and small, were noted on the map, the present-day tendency is to map only the risks involving larger liabilities, thus eliminating the detail of mapping small lines.

Prudent businessmen never put "all their eggs in one basket." Neither do fire insurance companies. Rather, they exercise careful judgment in order not to become too heavily involved in areas where one fire might result in destruction of an entire block or section of a community.

Because the maps show whether a building is constructed of wood, brick, steel and concrete, or any one of a number of other materials, each with different fire-resistive characteristics, they are an indispensable guide to company underwriters, who decide whether or not to accept all or part of a risk.

Role of Company "Examiner"

After the map clerk has made his notations at the appropriate location on the map, the daily report is turned over to an "examiner." It is up to him as an "underwriter" to

REPRESENTATIVE SAMPLE
OF A
SANBORN MAP

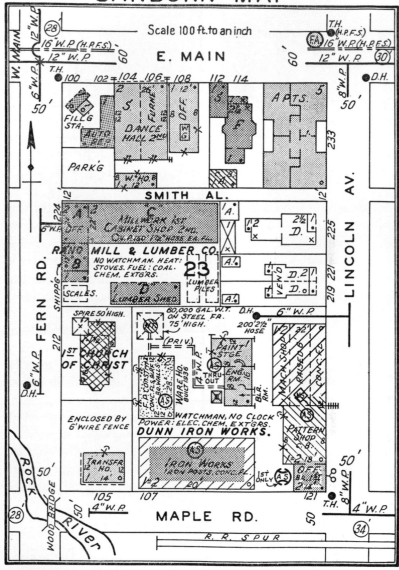

Scale 100 ft. to an inch

E. MAIN

SMITH AL.

W. MAIN

FERN RD.

LINCOLN AV.

MILL & LUMBER CO.
NO WATCHMAN. HEAT:
STOVES. FUEL: COAL.
CHEM. EXTGRS.

23

DUNN IRON WORKS.
WATCHMAN, NO CLOCK
POWER: ELEC. CHEM. EXTGRS.

1ST CHURCH OF CHRIST

ENCLOSED BY 6' WIRE FENCE

IRON WORKS

MAPLE RD.

R. R. SPUR

ROCK RIVER

WOOD BRIDGE

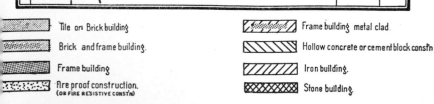

Tile or Brick building	Frame building metal clad.
Brick and frame building.	Hollow concrete or cement block constn
Frame building	Iron building.
Fire proof construction. (OR FIRE RESISTIVE CONSTN)	Stone building.

1. "DAILY REPORT" COMES FROM AGENT

2. MORAL HAZARD IS ANALYZED

3. MAP CLERK CHECKS PROPERTY

4. EXAMINER WEIGHS THE RISK

5. REINSURANCE IS ARRANGED

6. BOOKKEEPING DATA IS RECORDED

7. STATISTICIANS TABULATE DETAILS OF RISK

8. GEOGRAPHICAL FILING PERMITS READY REFERENCE

Progress of policy through company departments

weigh all the information available concerning the risk described in the daily report and then use his trained judgment in deciding how much insurance, if any, the company should accept.

Perhaps the daily report calls for fire insurance totaling $10,000 on a building in a block where the company has already assumed a relatively high amount of risk. Sound judgment may dictate that the company write no more than $5,000 on the new risk. Does that mean that the agent has to cancel the first policy for $10,000 and write two new policies for $5,000 each in a separate company?

Ordinarily, no; for the company may reinsure any portion of the risk that it does not care to retain for itself. Just as insurance is the arrangement by which an individual transfers his risks to a company, reinsurance is the device by which one company transfers to one or more other companies a part of the risks it has assumed. To provide for prompt and convenient handling of such risks, companies maintain reinsurance agreements with other organizations. Some organizations are set up solely as reinsurance companies, handling risks transferred to them from other companies rather than from individual property owners.

The examiner decides how much insurance his company will write on the properties described in the daily reports and how much liability should be transferred to other companies through reinsurance. The examiner always has available the counsel and advice of junior and senior underwriting executives and he confers with them daily.

Reinsurance thus represents an added measure of protection for policyholders. It reduces each company's liability for loss on any particular risk and is a graphic illustration of the principle of distribution of liability. In case of a loss, reinsurance does not affect the details of handling the claim settlement, which is the full responsibility of the company whose policy is held by the property owner.

The daily report is reviewed in several other departments before it is filed. It goes to the reinsurance department, where clerks make a record of the amount of risk that is being transferred; also to the bookkeeping and statistical departments, where information regarding the business done by the company is recorded.

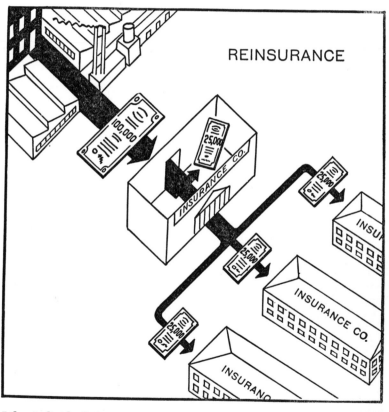

Like individual insures, insurance companies transfer part of their risks to other companies

After a property owner has received his policy from the agent, he may decide to increase the amount of insurance on his property or otherwise change the policy in a number of ways. These changes are made by the agent by means of endorsements attached to the original policy. These endorsements are printed or typewritten forms that are attached to, and become a part of, the policy.

Copies of the endorsements are sent to the company, where they are attached to the daily report in the company's files after being thoroughly checked in various departments.

At the end of the period of protection provided by the policy, the daily report is taken from the active files and placed with the inactive records. Some companies retain daily reports in this file for at least a year before destroying them. Usually the policyholder renews his insurance and, in such cases, the new daily reports, forwarded to the company by the agent, are checked carefully against the old ones.

Duties of Fieldmen

To assist its agents, companies maintain staffs of fieldmen, who serve as the contact between the company and its agents in a particular territory. The duties of these fieldmen are numerous. They inspect risks. They select and train agents. They help agents to keep abreast of new developments and new insurance needs of their policyholders. Because local agents usually represent more than one company, the fieldman endeavors, through demonstrations of useful service, to encourage each agent to give to his company an increasing share of the agency's business. Fieldmen have also become particularly helpful in planned fire prevention activities and in advising agents and policyholders regarding fire protection devices, individually and as members in field clubs and state fire prevention associations.

Security Behind the Promise

The most important element to the policyholder is the security behind his policies. Therefore the use to which a company puts the money it receives is vital to every property owner seeking protection.

When a local agent delivers a policy, he receives a payment, called a "premium", from the property owner. The amount of the premium is determined by multiplying the amount of insurance involved by the appropriate rate. An insurance rate is simply the cost of a unit of insurance, and the unit most generally used in property insurance is $100 of protection for a period of one year.

The rate applying to an ordinary residence, for instance, may be twenty-five cents. This means that the cost of protection is twenty-five cents for each $100 of insurance. If the owner of a house wanted to buy $10,000 of fire insurance, his premium would be $25 a year. Policies can also be written covering periods longer than one year, and the premium is subject to a reduction when term insurance is purchased.

How are fire insurance rates determined? Briefly, the underlying factor is the loss expectancy. Estimates of loss expectancy start with three fundamentals:

1. Previous experience involving many similar risks with particular emphasis on the occupancy involved.
2. The kind of building material used and the type of construction involved.
3. The extent and efficiency of public and private fire protection service, including the adequacy of the community's water supply.

The use to which a building may be put, its proximity to other buildings from which fires might spread, and a number of other factors also have a considerable bearing on insurance rates. Climatic and other characteristics also vary between states. Rates in each territory are generally established by special rating organizations that have had long years of experience in studying just such problems.

At the end of each month the agent sends to his companies a statement showing the amount of business he has written for them. He also sends to each company a check covering the amount of premiums due the company. Before making payment, the agent deducts his commission. From this commission the agent pays the costs of maintaining his local office, employees' salaries, and other business expenses.

Money received by the company is employed in various ways. First, of course, losses incurred under policies issued by the company must be met. Many types of taxes and fees must be set aside for Federal, state, and municipal authorities. In addition there is the very important item for salaries and home office expenses necessary to the conduct of the business.

The nature of the insurance business requires that companies maintain accounts to meet unforeseen as well as expected events. Two examples are the "loss reserve" and the "unearned premium reserve."

The loss reserve can be described as an account to reflect estimated liabilities for losses which have occurred. As notices of new losses are received, the account is increased, and as losses are paid, the account is reduced.

The unearned premium reserve is an account to record the premiums paid in advance and represents the money which would have to be paid back to policyholders should all policies be cancelled. The full amount of each premium paid to a company is not completely earned until expiration of the policy. At any time during the life of the policy the policyholder (or the company) has the right to cancel his insurance and demand the portion of his premium not yet earned by the company. The unearned premium thus represents the unexpired period of protection due the policyholder under his contract.

The function of all reserves is to safeguard policyholders.

11

The Insurance Adjuster

From the standpoint of the insurance buying public, one of the key men in the insurance business is the one who comes to adjust the loss—the adjuster.

The fair and prompt payment of losses is easy when the policyholder knows what the policy covers and understands that the basis of payment is actual cash value at the time of loss. Sometimes there are honest differences of opinion and the policy provides for appraisal. The percentage of fire insurance losses that cannot be settled without recourse either to appraisal or to the courts, however, is amazingly small—a tiny fraction of one percent.

The adjuster must be familiar with what the policy covers and skilled in the many complicated applications that arise in the course of his work. He has to be able to withstand unfair or exaggerated claims yet remain courteous and willing to pay the proper amount graciously. His is a difficult task.

Adjusting Organizations

Many companies have their own staff adjusters whom they send out to help determine and settle losses that occur to their policyholders. It is clearly impractical, however, for each company to have salaried adjusters in every section of the country where it might be called upon to adjust a loss. To make possible prompt and expert attention to policyholders' losses, the capital stock insurance companies maintain three adjusting organizations with over 725 claims offices throughout the United States and an adjusting staff of over 3000 adjusters. Many of these men are experts on particular kinds of property, such as chemical plants or textile factories. They must know values and keep abreast of the current cost of materials and labor. In addition to these company-owned adjusting organizations and staff adjusters, there is a third group known as independent adjusters whose services are available to the companies.

Salvage Facilities

The capital stock insurance companies maintain two salvage organizations, with countrywide facilities, for the reconditioning and disposal of damaged merchandise. Merchandise that may appear to be hopelessly destroyed many times has substantial value if properly reconditioned. In preserving these values, an important economic contribution is made in the conservation of property. The services of these salvage companies are available to all adjusters.

The Catastrophe Plan

Insurance has always been called upon to meet disaster. In order to bring prompt relief to policyholders in areas that have been devastated by conflagrations, explosions, hurricanes, tornadoes, windstorms or other disasters, the capital stock companies developed a catastrophe plan. Adjusters are rushed to the disaster area from all parts of the country and are organized for maximum efficiency and service to the policyholders under the catastrophe plan. A meeting is held with local contractors and repairmen to determine price guides for various types of repairs. This gives the adjusters a quick, working guide to local repair costs and helps the policyholder get prompt payment of his loss.

The plan has worked successfully in such different catastrophes as the Texas City explosion of 1947, the Florida-Gulf Coast hurricane of the same year, the Wichita hailstorm of 1953; Worcester, Massachusetts, Columbus, Georgia, and Waco, Texas, tornadoes of the same year, and the great Atlantic seaboard hurricanes, Carol and Edna in 1954.

Guiding Principles

The fire insurance business has also established a set of Guiding Principles that suggest how losses covered by "overlapping" policies will be apportioned between the companies. Whereas the policyholder is completely unaware of these suggested rules of procedure, they permit prompt and immediate payment, with the perplexities of apportionments resolved not at the time of loss but in anticipation of loss.

12

Fire Prevention—A Never-Ending Campaign

Every thirty-one seconds a fire will break out somewhere in this country. It may be a disastrous blaze consuming an entire section of a city. It may result in the deaths of many men, women and children and may injure or maim firemen. It may interrupt business and bring poverty and desolation in its wake. Or it may be a small fire in some home, easily controlled and extinguished after minor damage.

Close to one million fires, most of them preventable, occur each year in the United States. The value of the property destroyed by fire is staggering. It has been steadily increasing until it is now approaching one billion dollars a year.

In spite of the most efficient fire departments in the world, the United States wastes more money through property destroyed by fire than does any other nation. This situation is partly due to the fact that most American cities were built rapidly at a time when cheap, combustible materials were widely used. Wood has always been plentiful here and it was once used freely in the construction of walls, floors and roofs of nearly all buildings.

Fundamentally, a building of "fire-resistive construction" is one of such construction that it will remain structurally intact under severe fire conditions. Contents within this building, such as wooden desks and other office furniture, filing cabinets, paper and combustible stock, may be destroyed and the building may suffer considerable damage in a monetary sense but the structural framework, walls, floors and roof will not collapse.

Fire insurance alone cannot solve the problem of fire waste. Insurance cannot bring back property that has gone up in flames. It can indemnify a person for financial loss but all the insurance in the world cannot bring back to life the estimated 11,000 men, women and children whose deaths are caused by fire each year. It is no substitute for the hundreds of millions of dollars worth of homes, factories, schools, automobiles and personal belongings destroyed by fire every twelve months. The best type of protection against fire losses is fire prevention.

The National Board of Fire Underwriters

One of the leaders in the field of fire protection is the National Board of Fire Underwriters, a factual, engineering and educational organization maintained by the capital stock fire insurance companies, established in 1866. There are other excellent organizations active in the same field. However, since the National Board is the oldest and best known for its engineering standards and for the most continuous program of public service, its activities are outlined in this chapter to indicate the broad scope of organized fire prevention work in this country.

Typical of the thorough preventative efforts of the National Board, serving the interests of both its member companies and the nation, are the activities of its engineering department. Skilled engineers from this staff have made fire prevention surveys, later submitted as printed reports, of every city and town of more than 25,000 population in the country. Smaller communities receive the same type of survey by state or regional organizations maintained by the fire

insurance companies. The object of these surveys, made
without cost to the communities involved, is to detect conditions that might cause preventable fires or make it difficult
to fight fires caused by uncontrollable factors. The surveys
are repeated at intervals.

Safety is the full-time concern of engineers drawn from many fields

Working in groups of three or four, each man a specialist
in a particular phase of fire prevention or fire fighting, these
engineers spend from a week to several months studying fire
hazards in each principal city from coast to coast and in our
territorial possessions. The recommendations resulting from
these thorough surveys are transmitted to local municipal
officials for their consideration and action. They are also
studied by civil authorities to determine how well cities are
equipped to face a bombing attack or the results of an atomic
explosion and for other purposes.

The engineers study the water supply upon which a city
depends when fighting a fire; they conduct flow tests on fire
hydrants in various sections of the city to be certain the
pressure and quantities are adequate. The hydrant nearest

ALL CITIES AND
TOWNS ARE INSPECTED

CHECKING WATER SUPPLY

STUDYING FIRE
DEPARTMENT EFFICIENCY

Fire prevention experts

your home may have been inspected the last time these engineers studied conditions in your community. They check the ability of the men in the fire department, the efficiency of the trucks, engines, and other equipment; and they inspect the fire alarm system. Since building construction is an important factor in fire prevention, this, together with building codes and fire prevention ordinances, is carefully analyzed. Hundreds of individual subjects, each one related to some problem of fire fighting or fire prevention, are considered before the final report of the engineering crew is drafted.

Making Buildings Safer

Fire prevention should begin before a home or factory is even built. Obviously, a building so planned that it will contain a minimum of fire hazards is less of a fire prevention problem than a structure built haphazardly. The type of material used in a building is an important factor. While no building can be made 100

per cent "fireproof", use of
materials that have a high degree of resistance to fire can
reduce conflagration hazards
appreciably.

For the promotion of this
objective, facilities devoted
solely to problems connected
with the construction of buildings are maintained. As long
ago as 1905, a model building
code was prepared by the National Board of Fire Underwriters and first offered to the
public. Revised periodically,
this National Building Code is
used throughout the country
by municipal officials, archi-
tects, contractors, and educa-
tors. Perhaps it is being en-
forced in your own community
right now.

Work With Public Officials

Competent advice and practical assistance is made available to fire department officials
on matters relating to new
methods of preventing and
fighting fires. Reports on new
hazards in many types of industries have provided innu-
merable factory owners and
merchants with the best scien-

RECOMMENDING ELIMI-
NATION OF FIRE HAZARDS

ADVISING ON IMPROVE-
MENT OF BUILDING CODES

FIGHTING ARSON
NATIONWIDE

Helping public officials

tific knowledge that is available for the protection of their properties.

The services of trained experts are constantly at the disposal of the United States Government and the governments of the states and cities. Fire prevention engineers played an important part in reducing losses from fire in government warehouses, dock properties, camps, ammunition depots, and throughout government property generally during both World Wars. They advised on the planning and construction of government properties and examined countless factories producing the sinews of war.

Close contact is also maintained with all other city officials whose duties involve any of the various phases of fire prevention and fire extinguishment.

Criminals who burn property maliciously are responsible for the loss of many lives and the destruction of much valuable property. This crime, technically known as "arson," is difficult to detect. The more successful it is, the better it destroys its own evidence. Unlike other crimes, which occur with a certain degree of regularity in most communities, arson may not occur in a given town for many years. Thus it would be highly expensive for the average town or small city to support special arson detectives.

To aid in the solution of this problem, a nation-wide arson department is maintained by the National Board of Fire Underwriters. It employs a corps of trained investigators, located at key points in every section of the country, ready to help local police departments, fire prevention officials, and other law-enforcement officers. Operating without regard to whether or not the property involved is insured, arson department special agents have helped bring hundreds of criminals to justice.

Hijackers and jewel and fur thieves often operate on an

interstate basis. Many move from one popular resort to another with the seasons. National Board investigators have made themselves expert on the more dangerous thieves and gangs and their methods; and have assembled picture files not only of the criminals but of their loot. These agents give made themselves expert on the more dangerous thieves and not only of the criminals but of their loot. These agents give valuable aid to local authorities in their efforts to suppress these crimes. In this way, the insurance business makes a contribution to the peace and security of the entire community.

13

Fire Prevention Throughout the Community

The most horrible fires are those occurring in schools and hospitals. Most of these tragedies could be prevented if the buildings were examined carefully and regularly with the aim of exposing unnecessary fire hazards. The National Board has prepared special self-inspection blanks to enable school and hospital authorities to recognize and eliminate many conditions that might breed fires. Following two terrible hospital fires, the fire and casualty insurance companies aided by hospital and other groups, made an inspection of all of the 6,800 hospitals in the United States and provided without charge professional advice on their alarm systems, fire fighting methods, plans for evacuation of patients, general housekeeping and the fire resistant quality of their buildings.

Hundreds of thousands of Home Fire Safety check lists are used each year in local programs designed to expose and correct fire hazards in the home.

Cities and towns in many states have adopted the Fire Prevention Code prepared by fire protection engineers of the National Board of Fire Underwriters. By enacting and enforcing this code, municipalities are able to reduce both the number and serious nature of many fire hazards that otherwise might go undetected. Immediately following the tragic Cocoanut Grove night-club fire in Boston, Massachusetts, on November 28, 1942, in which nearly 500 persons lost their lives, a special fire prevention ordinance applying to life safety in places of public assembly was prepared to help the many communities that suddenly awakened to the need for more adequate fire prevention measures.

The President's Conference on Fire Prevention in 1947 succeeded in further stimulating widespread interest in fire prevention problems by leading citizens in a great number of fields outside fire departments and fire insurance. This Conference was followed by other meetings in most of the states, dedicated to developing a sense of local responsibility for preventing the terrible toll of lives and property caused by fire every year.

Fire Prevention Education

In a long range program of fire prevention, the education of children has top importance. A vast amount of fire prevention education is conducted in the schools with the active cooperation and assistance both of local fire departments and national groups. Among the materials used by

Surprise fire drills help to prevent panic

teachers are audio-visual programs made available by the National Commission for Safety Education of the National Education Association. The last few years have seen fire safety brought into the everyday educational activities of the schools in a way that has never been done before.

The National Board assists local fire prevention efforts throughout the country. It provides materials for use by newspapers, radio and television stations, and distributes millions of pieces of fire safety literature, self-inspection blanks for homes, hospitals, factories, and other properties. This broad plan for safety to life and fire prevention is also carried on by means of films suitable for group or television showing, radio shorts and advertising material for use by local agents and brokers.

Research On New Fire Causes

With each advance in the technique of modern industry and modern living, come changes in methods and materials which require a new and expert look into the fire hazards that may be created. A Research Division of the National Board of Fire Underwriters is devoted to studying such situations. It issues technical booklets on industrial fire subjects and reports for more general consumption on such subjects as the fire hazards in various industries and the fire prevention problems of atomic energy cyclotrons and nuclear power plants.

Research Division engineers also rush to the scene of major fire and explosion disasters to get the facts first hand and present an impartial report on what happened and what caused the catastrophe and how such a disaster might be prevented elsewhere. The Texas City explosion, the terrifying series of gas explosions that wrecked suburban homes in Brighton, New York, and the Holland Tunnel fire are typical of the subjects covered by these reports.

"Fire Prevention Week"

One of the most widely promoted special "weeks" is Fire Prevention Week, a major project of the National Board and all other leading fire prevention organizations. Special proclamations and observances are centered around the anniversary of the Chicago Fire, October 9, 1871. Fire Prevention Week has been proclaimed officially by each President of the United States since 1922. Today it is marked by special articles in newspapers, magazines and a wide variety of types of publications; by programs on radio and television.

Spring Clean-Up Week is another project closely related to the problems of fire prevention and is observed widely throughout the United States and Canada each year.

Underwriters' Laboratories, Inc.

Just as fire prevention should begin with the construction of buildings so should it also be considered in the manufacture of all articles that might cause a fire or fail to retard one. The problem is to determine which products are safe from a fire prevention standpoint and which are potential fire hazards. For more than sixty years the answers to this problem have been supplied by Underwriters' Laboratories, Inc., a non-profit service organization with headquarters in Chicago. This unparalleled institution is maintained solely to test articles for their ability to protect life and property from the hazards of fire, accident and crime. In addition to the seventeen departmental laboratories occupying more than three acres of floor space in Chicago, Underwriters' Laboratories, Inc., maintains testing stations in New York City; Santa Clara, California; and Northbrook, Illinois; plus nearly 200 inspection centers throughout the United States.

It has tested the products of thousands of manufacturers in basic industries. Although roughly half of all products examined are rejected on the first test, Underwriters' Labora-

tories has listed hundreds of thousands of products—from oil
burners and lamp cords to roofing materials and television
sets. Articles that meet the specified requirements are permitted to display distinctive markings.

A familiar Underwriters' Laboratories label

The manufacturer pays a fee for the tests, whether his
product "passes" or not. When a product is rejected, the
manufacturer receives a detailed report, showing just which
safety specifications the device failed to meet. In some
cases only minor changes are required to bring the product
up to standard. When those changes have been made, the
manufacturer may then send the article back for a second
test. A unique feature is the further continuous check-up
on the manufacture of such commercial products and materials destined for use by the public.

Established by member companies of the National Board,
Underwriters' Laboratories is now self-supporting although
the Board continues to act as its sponsor.

Other Fire Prevention Organizations

Much effective fire prevention activity is carried on by
other national organizations whose membership includes not
only insurance people but a broad cross section of American
industry. One of the most interesting is the National Fire
Protection Association, whose membership is open to anyone
concerned with the problems of reducing fire waste. The

Association enjoys the support of engineers and technical experts of many industries interested in fire hazards and prevention methods. The resulting advisory publications, field visits and wide publicity stimulate public interest.

The National Fire Waste Council includes representatives of several governmental bureaus and of approximately twenty national organizations. Established by the Chamber of Commerce of the United States to secure the cooperation of local chambers of commerce in continuous fire prevention activities, the Council now conducts the Inter-Chamber Fire Waste Contest each year.

The International Association of Fire Chiefs, the National Safety Council, the Railway Fire Protection Association and the Society of Fire Protection Engineers, a new professional organization in the field, are other organizations actively engaged in this work.

The United States Department of Agriculture, the United States Bureau of Standards, and the United States Forest Service have done notable work in promoting fire safety. The Federal Fire Council was established in 1930 to help government departments in their efforts to reduce fire loss. State and local governments have also contributed substantially to this work through the enactment of special fire prevention programs.

14

Opportunities For Careers In Property Insurance

Insurance is more than just a business, a university president has pointed out. "Insurance is a part of and a contributor to the civilization of our time and in a high degree produces the sense of security and confidence which makes for satisfaction in living."

To anyone debating the choice of a career, the property insurance business is one whose social worth stands high among the business activities of the nation. It is a business that, in addition to the prestige that comes from worthwhile service, offers to those who are part of it unusual security and permanence. The protection of insurance runs like a thread through our business and personal lives.

The business offers exceptional stability. Because men throughout the ages have continued to seek peace of mind through the transfer of personal and business risks, this stability has not been seriously affected by wars, revolutions or social changes. Many business activities change from one generation to another. Mechanical refrigeration has revolutionized the ice industry. Busses, trucks and planes have changed the picture of modern transportation. Many other examples could be cited. But throughout all these changes, the need for protection has made of insurance a sturdy, permanent institution, which has expanded constantly to meet changing conditions and needs.

Insurance is an institution of service. Insurance men and women perform an important social service to the community. Through them many people have been able to realize their desire for financial security and progress. Through them the credit system of our nation has been strengthened.

Property insurance is a factor in the operation of every industry and in the lives of all persons. They may be merchants or clerks, manufacturers or mechanics, teachers

Every type of property owner benefits from the skilled service of the insurance agent

or students. However great or small their wealth or social position, they all need protection against the loss of their possessions. Insurance helps in the operation of railroad systems, steel mills, farms and cities. The person who chooses a career in property insurance becomes, in a very real sense, a partner in the nation's progress.

There is a place in the industry for the application of almost every business skill.

Opportunities in Company Organizations

Insurance companies offer many interesting job opportunities for men and women. An insurance company office is a nerve center of the business. Into it pour the thousands of transfers of risks which have been arranged by agents and brokers throughout the country. Each day brings new problems. How can protection best be provided for some huge aviation plant in the South—or for some large chain of food stores in the Northwest? What recommendations could be made to reduce the hazards of operating a sawmill in a remote logging camp? What is the soundest way of handling the insurance on a collection of "priceless" paintings in some famous museum?

Always, of course, one basic question must be answered: "Should this risk be accepted and, if so, for how much?" The answer can be given only by experienced underwriters, the key employees in insurance company operations.

Underwriters are guided by information reaching them from many different sources. From a company's own engineers may come special reports concerning the hazards in a particular property. Other detailed engineering reports may be received from rating bureaus, which inspect property in a specific territory and develop insurance rates for various types of buildings.

From fieldmen, salaried traveling representatives of the

company, may come additional information. Credit agencies may be asked for special reports on the character and financial standing of the property owner. Data developed by fire prevention experts may also be considered. Thus the work of trained men in many branches of the business contributes to the underwriter's knowledge of the risk. Upon this knowledge is based his judgment of the acceptability of the risk.

Underwriting is only one field of activity in an insurance company office. Accounting and bookkeeping are exceptionally important functions in a business that depends so largely on accurate records of financial transactions. The accounting department is usually one of the largest in the average property insurance company and offers many job opportunities.

Money in the various funds of a property insurance company must be invested in sound, productive enterprises to yield income that will help meet the costs of operating the organization. Thus the operations of the investment department are of prime importance to the average company and require the services of financial experts with a wide range of knowledge in many fields.

Purchasing and supply departments, personnel departments, which offer career opportunities to copywriters, artists, research workers, and experts in other phases of promotional activity. One important function of such departments is that of providing helpful advertising material for agents representing the company.

Purchasing and supply departments, personnel departments, educational departments, statistical departments and business development departments are integral parts of many companies.

Numerous interesting jobs are also available to the one who qualifies as an adjuster, working as a salaried employee

SOME VOCATIONAL OPPORTUNITIES IN PROPERTY INSURANCE COMPANIES

UNDERWRITING

ADMINISTRATIVE

ENGINEERING

AGENCY
SUPERVISION

FIELD
CONTACTS

BOOKKEEPING-
STATISTICAL

PERSONNEL

LOSS
SETTLEMENT

FILING, TYPING

EDUCATIONAL

SALES PROMOTION

INVESTMENTS

of a company or on the staff of an adjustment bureau maintained by the companies, or as an independent adjuster working for himself.

Agents and Brokers

Agents and brokers possess a rare asset, independence. They are their own bosses. They have complete freedom to select the people with whom to do business. They are free to create ideas and plans and to fulfill them.

Certain fundamental requirements are necessary to the success of an agent or a broker. He must have imagination. He must be able to visualize insurance problems and reach correct solutions. He must be able to think in terms of the services insurance can perform for his clients and prospective clients.

An agent must have enthusiasm and the ability to present his ideas clearly and effectively. He must be capable of self-management; he must be able to "plan his work and work his plans" without wasting time or energy. Because he is part of a constantly changing business, he must be willing to learn and keep abreast of the times.

Educational Courses

Young men or women who wish to follow a career in property insurance will find many avenues of training open to them. Courses covering numerous phases of the business are now available in leading colleges and schools of business throughout the country. In large cities specialized training is frequently offered by insurance societies.* For the benefit of those who are unable to attend class sessions, a comprehensive series of correspondence courses are available.

---

* A list of insurance societies offering educational facilities appears in Appendix B, page 109.

Many local associations of insurance agents throughout the country also conduct training courses by national authorities to cover the fundamentals of the business and its basic operating principles.

There is no better way to appreciate the opportunities offered by property insurance than to become a part of the business itself. Local agencies and companies both offer opportunities to begin interesting careers. Individual agents in your community, or officers of the local association of insurance agents, should be consulted for the answers to specific questions concerning the business.

For the youth with vision and ability, property insurance offers many promising opportunities. As a company underwriter he will face the challenge of a wide variety of risks every business day. His competence may be the deciding factor not only in the success of his company but in the continuing security of many individuals or enterprises. As a local agent or broker he may be called upon to provide proper insurance protection for a business vital to the community or for a factory supplying materials vital to the nation.

Whatever his job, he will have the satisfaction of knowing that he is part of an institution of recognized social worth that is daily bringing peace of mind to millions of property owners. He will be a part of a vital business that has made an outstanding contribution to our nation's growth.

Interesting Property Insurance Terms

P roperty insurance, like every other business, has many special terms that may not be clearly understood by those outside the business. The following glossary is designed to acquaint the reader with a number of distinctive terms commonly used in the business.

While the definitions submitted may leave something to be desired from a legal or technical point of view, they are adequate for the purpose of the book, which is to introduce the reader to a general understanding of property insurance.

Abandonment. The owner of property that has been damaged may seek to surrender his property to the company for the purpose of claiming a total loss. This is not permitted under the terms of the fire insurance policy, or most property insurance contracts.

Acquisition Cost. Generally refers to commissions paid to agents and brokers.

Actual Cash Value. Usually means the sum of money required at the time of a loss to replace the property destroyed, less wear and tear and depreciation for previous use. Many factors, such as the nature of the property and the market value of the property, may be involved in determining the actual cash value of an individual loss.

Additional Extended Coverage Endorsement. An endorsement extending the fire policy to which an Extended Coverage Endorsement has been attached to cover accidental discharge, leakage or overflow of water or steam; sudden and accidental tearing asunder, cracking, burning or bulging of a steam or hot water heating or storage system; vandalism and malicious mischief; vehicles owned or operated by the insured or by a tenant of the described premises; fall of trees; objects falling from the weight of ice, snow or sleet; freezing of plumbing, heating and air conditioning systems and domestic appliances; collapse of building(s); landslide; breakage of glass.

Adjuster. The company representative who deals with the property owner in the adjustment of a loss.

Agent. An insurance agent, frequently referred to as a local agent, is an independent representative of an insurance company. He is the sales and service representative of the company, and is paid on a commission basis. He is licensed by the state in which he operates. A state agent or special agent is an employee of the company. He serves as the personal contact between the company and its agents in a given territory. A general agent (or general agency) is an independent person, or corporation, authorized by a company to appoint and supervise agents for the company in a given territory and receiving compensation on a commission basis.

All Risk Insurance. Protects the property covered against loss from all perils except those specifically excluded by the terms of the policy. This contrasts with the usual policy which names the peril or perils insured against.

American Agency System. The practice of selling insurance through independent local agents on a commission basis.

Appraisal. An estimate of the value of property, made by impartial experts.

Arson. The wilful and malicious burning of property, sometimes with the intent of defrauding insurance companies.

Assignment. The transfer of the legal right or interest in a policy to another party, generally in connection with the sale of property.

Authorization. Agents and brokers frequently submit risks to companies to determine how much insurance the company is willing to write on a given property. The amount of insurance the company agrees to write is known as an "authorization."

Binder. A temporary agreement given to a property owner who desires insurance, "binding" the company to pay the loss if damage from the peril insured against should occur before the policy is written.

Blanket Policy. A broad type of coverage. A "blanket" policy covers different types of property, such as buildings, machinery, and stocks of merchandise at one or more locations and specifies one aggregate amount of coverage.

Broker. An insurance broker is a solicitor of insurance who does not represent insurance companies in a capacity as agent but places orders for coverage with companies designated by the insured or with companies of his own choosing. In most circumstances he is the agent of the insured.

Business Interruption Insurance. (Also known as Use and Occupancy Insurance.) This type of insurance is designed to protect the property owner against loss of earnings resulting from the interruption of a business as a consequence of perils insured against.

Capital Stock Insurance Company. A company having, in addition to surplus and reserve funds, a capital fund paid in by stockholders.

Coinsurance. A policy provision or endorsement specifying that the property owner will carry insurance amounting to at least a stated percentage of the value of the property in consideration of a reduced rate.

Commission. Insurance agents and brokers are usually compensated by being allowed to retain a certain percentage of the premiums they produce. Such an allowance is known as "commission."

Commissioners. State officials charged with enforcement of statutes pertaining to insurance business. In some instances titles of these officials differ. In New York State, for example, the official is known as the Superintendent of Insurance.

Consequential Loss. Standard fire policies cover against "direct" loss resulting from the destruction of the property by fire. Indirect losses, as a consequence of physical damage to property by fire, are not infrequent. Such losses are described as "consequential losses." For example, loss of earnings or income from property.

Daily Report. An abbreviated copy of the policy mailed to the company by the agent, who usually retains a second copy for his records.

Depreciation. Decrease in the value of property over a period of time due to wear and tear or obsolescence.

Endorsement. Special circumstances frequently require that a policy be altered. Such alterations are effected by attaching to the policy a form bearing the language necessary to record the change.

Expense Ratio. The ratio of operating expenses (including taxes and commissions to agents and brokers) to premiums.

Exposure. Property subject to damage caused by spread of risk, such as fire, beyond the building of origin.

Extended Coverage Endorsement. An endorsement extending the fire policy to cover loss caused by windstorm, hail, explosion, riot, riot attending a strike, civil commotion, aircraft, vehicles, and smoke.

Fire Marshal. Public official charged with the prevention and investigation of fires.

Fireproof—(Fire-resistive). The term "fireproof" is a misnomer. Fire occurring in an adjoining building or in the combustible contents of a building may cause damage to any structure. Therefore no building can accurately be termed "fireproof." The term "fire-resistive" is a more precise definition describing modern construction designed to resist fires.

Floater Policy. A policy under the terms of which protection follows movable property, covering it wherever it may be; for example, a policy on tourist's baggage.

Form. A descriptive form attached to a policy setting forth the nature of the property covered, the location, and other pertinent data. It may grant certain privileges or impose certain obligations on the insured.

Hazard. This term is applied to conditions which may create or increase considerably the probability that a loss due to a given peril may occur.

Inland Marine Insurance. A type of insurance, broad in scope, generally covering articles that may be transported from one place to another.

Insurable Interest. Any interest in property—or any legal relation to it—of such a nature that a contemplated peril might cause monetary loss to the insured.

Insured. The person, partnership, or corporation in whose name the policy is written.

Insurer. One who accepts an insurance risk.

"Line." Colloquial term with several meanings. It may be used in connection with a particular type of insurance. ("Agent Jones writes the fire line on the Ajax Building.") It may also be used to describe all the various types of insurance written for a property owner. ("The Ajax Company line is handled by the Jones Agency.") The term is sometimes used to describe the amount of insurance on a given property. ("The Jones Agency has a $10,000 line on the Ajax Company garage.")

Local Agent. (See Agent.)

Moral Hazard. In contrast to physical hazards, moral hazards are character risks that are difficult to chart. For example, an individual or firm with a long record of suspicious fires presents an increased moral hazard.

Multiple Line. Combining insurance of different types such as fire and liability—a "multiple line policy" or a "multiple line company."

Peril. This term refers to the causes of possible loss, for instance: fire, windstorm, explosion, and the like.

Policy. The written contract of insurance.

Premium.   The sum paid for a policy of insurance.

Proof of Loss.   A formal statement of a claim for payment of a loss made by an insured to an insurance company.

Protection.   (1) Term used interchangeably with the word "coverage" to denote the insurance provided under the terms of a policy.   (2) Term used to indicate the existence of fire-fighting facilities in an area known as as a "protected" area.

Rate.   The cost of a unit of insurance.   Fire insurance rates are usually quoted in terms of $100 of insurance for a period of one year.

Rating Bureau or Organization.   An organization that compiles data and measures hazards of individual risks in terms of rates in a given territory.

Reinsurance.   The practice of insurance companies of distributing among other companies the excess liability above the amount which the original company desires to retain.

Rider.   Term sometimes given to an endorsement.   (See Endorsement.)

Risk.   (1) Any chance of loss.   (2) The individual or the property to which an insurance policy relates.

Salvage.   The value of property after it has been damaged by fire or other perils.

Subrogation.   The legal process by which an insurance company seeks from a third party who may have caused the loss, recovery of the amount paid to the policyholder.

Underwriter.   A key employee of an insurance company whose duty it is to determine the acceptability of risks.   Also an insurance company.

Use and Occupancy Insurance.   (See Business Interruption Insurance.)

APPENDIX B

Sources of Property Insurance Information and Education

I. Your property insurance agent and your property insurance company, whose names and addresses appear on each policy.

II. American Institute for property and Liability Underwriters, Inc., 3924 Walnut Street, Philadelphia 4, Pennsylvania. This institute was organized to sponsor and advance the cause of property insurance education at the collegiate level. It provides yearly examinations leading to the degree of "Chartered Property and Casualty Underwriter." Students prepare for these examinations by participating in insurance courses in many universities or in study groups in individual communities.

III. Insurance Institute of America, 3924 Walnut Street, Philadelphia 4, Pennsylvania, makes available a program of study in property and casualty insurance designed for those who wish to obtain a broad and basic knowledge of the business. The institute does not conduct courses, but supplies study guides on the material covered in its three examinations. These examinations are given twice yearly throughout the United States, and those who pass them receive the final Certificate of the Insurance Institute of America.

IV. National Association of Insurance Agents, Educational Division, 96 Fulton Street, New York 38, New York

V. Insurance Library Association of Boston, 89 Broad Street,
    Boston, Massachusetts

    Insurance Library Association of Atlanta, 1030 Hurt Build-
    ing, Atlanta 3, Georgia

    Insurance Society of Philadelphia, 232 South Fourth Street,
    Philadelphia, Pennsylvania

    Insurance Society of New York, Inc., 225 Broadway, New
    York 7, New York; Library: 107 William Street, New
    York 38, New York

    Insurance Library of Chicago, 175 West Jackson Boulevard,
    Chicago, Illinois

    Fire Underwriters Association of the Pacific, 215 Battery
    Street, San Francisco, California

    Some of these organizations sponsor courses in insurance
    and in some cases maintain extensive insurance libraries
    open to the public.

VI. Chamber of Commerce of the United States, Insurance
     Department, 1615 H Street, N.W., Washington 6, D.C.

VII. American Association of University Teachers of Insurance,
      c/o Dean William Beadles, Illinois Wesleyan University,
      Bloomington, Illinois.

APPENDIX C

Reading List

ADJUSTMENT OF PROPERTY INSURANCE LOSSES by Prentiss B. Reed. McGraw-Hill, New York. 2nd edition, 1953. 667 pages

AGENT'S KEY TO FIRE INSURANCE by Robert P. Barbour. Chilton Publications, Philadelphia. 6th edition, 1949. 649 pages

AS YOU PASS BY by Kenneth H. Dunshee. Hastings House, New York 1952. 270 pages

BUSINESS INTERRUPTION INSURANCE by Henry C. Klein, Rough Notes, Indianapolis, Indiana. Edition 1950

DICTIONARY OF INSURANCE TERMS by Ralph Blanchard. Chamber of Commerce of U.S., Washington. 1949. 74 pages

DISASTER ON YOUR DOORSTEP by Paul W. Kearney. Harper, New York. 1953. 210 pages

FIRE INSURANCE by Robert S. Riegel and Jerome S. Miller. Prentice-Hall, New York. 1949

FIRES AND FIRE FIGHTERS by John V. Morris. Little, Brown. Boston. 1955. 393 pages

FIRE, CASUALTY & SURETY BULLETINS. National Underwriter, Cincinnati

FIRE INSURANCE INSPECTION AND UNDERWRITING by Walter O. Lincoln, George W. Tisdale and John W. Babcock. Chilton Publications, Philadelphia. 7th edition

FIRE INSURANCE UNDERWRITING by Prentiss B. Reed. McGraw-Hill, New York. 1940. 380 pages

FIRE PREVENTION CODE National Board of Fire Underwriters, New York. 1953. 189 pages

GENERAL INSURANCE by John H. Magee. Irwin, Homewood, Illinois. 1953

GOING TO BLAZES by Robert V. Masters. Sterling, New York. 1950. 143 pages

INSURANCE, ITS THEORY AND PRACTICE IN THE UNITED STATES by Albert H. Mowbray and Ralph H. Blanchard. McGraw-Hill, New York. 4th edition. 1955. 549 pages

INSURANCE, PRINCIPLES AND COVERAGES by George G. R. Lucas and Ralph H. Wherry. Rinehart, New York. 1954

INSURANCE PRINCIPLES AND PRACTICES by Robert S. Riegel and Jerome S. Miller. Prentice-Hall, New York. 1947. 788 pages

INSURANCE WORDS AND THEIR MEANINGS by Vincent L. Gallagher. Rough Notes, Indianapolis. 1954. 90 pages

INTRODUCTION TO INSURANCE by Laurence E. Falls. Insurance Institute of America, New York. 1949. 94 pages

KNOW YOUR FIRE INSURANCE AND EXTENDED COVERAGE by E. E. Demarest. Canyon Press, New York. 1951. 94 pages

POLICY FORM AND MANUAL ANALYSIS SERVICE. Rough Notes, Indianapolis

PRIMER ON ADJUSTMENTS by William C. Moore. Rough Notes, Indianapolis

PRINCIPLES OF INSURANCE by John H. Magee. Irwin, Homewood, Illinois. 1947. 725 pages

PRINCIPLES OF INSURANCE by Mehr and Cammack. Irwin, Homewood, Illinois. 1952. 779 pages

PROPERTY & CASUALTY INSURANCE by P. Gordis. Rough Notes, Indianapolis. 1953

PROPERTY INSURANCE by John H. Magee. Irwin, Homewood, Illinois. Third edition 1955

PROPERTY INSURANCE by S. S. Huebner with G. L. Amrhein and C. A. Kline. D. Appleton Century, New York. Third edition 1938. 682 pages

625 QUESTIONS AND ANSWERS ON FIRE AND MARINE INSURANCE. United States Review Publishing Co., Philadelphia

YOUR PERSONAL INSURANCE GUIDE by Jerome S. Miller. Simon & Schuster, New York. 1955. 322 pages

APPENDIX D

INSURANCE FORMS shown on following pages

Standard Fire Insurance Policy
Extended Coverage Indorsement No. 4
Additional Extended Coverage Indorsement

No.

RENEWAL OF No.

National Association
INSURANCE COMPANY
NEW YORK, N. Y.

INSURANCE IS PROVIDED AGAINST ONLY THOSE PERILS AND FOR ONLY THOSE COVERAGES INDICATED BELOW BY A PREMIUM CHARGE AND AGAINST OTHER PERILS AND FOR OTHER COVERAGES ONLY WHEN ENDORSED HEREON OR ADDED HERETO.

PERIL(S) Insured Against and Cover-
age(s) Provided (Insert Name of Each)

	AMOUNT	RATE	PREMIUM
FIRE AND LIGHTNING	$	$	$
EXTENDED COVERAGE X X X X X X X X X X X X X	$	$	$
		$	$
		$	$

TOTAL PREMIUM $

IN CONSIDERATION OF THE PROVISIONS AND STIPULATIONS HEREIN OR ADDED HERETO
AND OF the premium above specified, this Company, for the term of   from
At Noon (Standard Time) to   At Noon (Standard Time)
at location of property involved, to an amount not exceeding the amount(s) above specified, does insure

and legal representatives, to the extent of the actual cash value of the property at the time of loss, but not exceeding the amount which it would cost to repair or replace the property with material of like kind and quality within a reasonable time after such loss, without allowance

DIRECT LOSS BY FIRE, LIGHTNING AND BY REMOVAL FROM PREMISES ENDANGERED BY THE PERILS INSURED AGAINST IN THIS POLICY, EXCEPT AS HEREINAFTER PROVIDED, to the property described hereinafter while located or contained as described in this policy, or pro rata for five days at each proper place to which any of the property shall necessarily be removed for preservation from the perils insured against in this policy, but not elsewhere.

1 Item No.	Amount Fire or Fire and Extended Coverage, or Other Peril	2 Per Cent of Co-Insurance Applicable	Amount Other Peril If Different Than Fire	3 Per Cent of Co-Insurance Applicable	4 DESCRIPTION AND LOCATION OF PROPERTY COVERED Show construction, type of roof and occupancy of building(s) covered or containing the property covered. If occupied as a dwelling state No. of families.

Subject to Form No(s)._____ INSERT FORM NUMBER(s) AND EDITION DATE(s)_____ attached hereto.

Mortgage Clause: Subject to the provisions of the mortgage clause attached hereto, loss, if any, on building items, shall be payable to:

Assignment of this policy shall not be valid except with the written consent of this Company.
This policy is made and accepted subject to the foregoing provisions and stipulations and those hereinafter stated, which are hereby made a part of this policy, together with such other provisions, stipulations and agreements as may be added hereto, as provided in this policy.

Agency at

Countersignature Date _____ Agent

1 Concealment,
2 fraud.
3
This entire policy shall be void if, whether before or after a loss, the insured has wilfully concealed or misrepresented any ma-

4 terial fact or circumstance concerning this insurance or the
5 subject thereof, or the interest of the insured therein, or in case
6 of any fraud or false swearing by the insured relating thereto.

7 Uninsurable
8 and
9 excepted property.
10
This policy shall not cover accounts, bills, currency, deeds, evidences of debt, money or securities; nor, unless specifically named herein in writing, bullion or manuscripts.

11 Perils not
12 included.
13
This Company shall not be liable for loss by fire or other perils insured against in this policy caused, directly or indirectly, by: (a)

14 enemy attack by armed forces, including action taken by mili-
15 tary, naval or air forces in resisting an actual or an immediately
16 impend'ag enemy attack; (b) invasion; (c) insurrection; (d)
17 rebellion; (e) revolution; (f) civil war; (g) usurped power; (h)
18 order of any civil authority except acts of destruction at the time
19 of and for the purpose of preventing the spread of fire, provided
20 that such fire did not originate from any of the perils excluded
21 by this policy; (i) neglect of the insured to use all reasonable
22 means to save and preserve the property at and after a loss, or
23 when the property is endangered by fire in neighboring prem-
24 ises; (j) nor shall this Company be liable for loss by theft.

25 Other Insurance.
26
Other insurance may be prohibited or the amount of insurance may be limited by en-

27 dorsement attached hereto.

28 Conditions suspending or restricting insurance. Unless other-
29 wise provided in writing added hereto this Company shall not
30 be liable for loss occurring

31 (a) while the hazard is increased by any means within the con-
32 trol or knowledge of the insured; or
33 (b) while a described building, whether intended for occupancy
34 by owner or tenant, is vacant or unoccupied beyond a period of
35 sixty consecutive days; or
36 (c) as a result of explosion or riot, unless fire ensue, and in
37 that event for loss by fire only.

38 Other perils
39 or subjects.
Any other peril to be insured against or subject of insurance to be covered in this policy shall be by endorsement in writing hereon or

40 shall be by endorsement in writing hereon or
41 added hereto.

42 Added provisions.
43
The extent of the application of insurance under this policy and of the contribution to

44 be made by this Company in case of loss, and any other pro-
45 vision or agreement not inconsistent with the provisions of this
46 policy, may be provided for in writing added hereto, but no pro-

84 relating to the interests and obligations of such mortgagee may
85 be added hereto by agreement in writing.
86 Pro rata liability. This Company shall not be liable for a greater
87 proportion of any loss than the amount
88 hereby insured shall bear to the whole insurance covering the
89 property against the peril involved, whether collectible or not.
90 Requirements in The insured shall give immediate written
91 case loss occurs. notice to this Company of any loss, protect
92 the property from further damage, forthwith
93 separate the damaged and undamaged personal property, put
94 it in the best possible order, furnish a complete inventory of
95 the destroyed, damaged and undamaged property, showing in
96 detail quantities, costs, actual cash value and amount of loss
97 claimed; and within sixty days after the loss, unless such time
98 is extended in writing by this Company, the insured shall render
99 to this Company a proof of loss, signed and sworn to by the
100 insured, stating the knowledge and belief of the insured as to
101 the following: the time and origin of the loss, the interest of the
102 insured and of all others in the property, the actual cash value of
103 each item thereof and the amount of loss thereto, all encum-
104 brances thereon, all other contracts of insurance, whether valid
105 or not, covering any of said property, any changes in the title,
106 use, occupation, location, possession or exposures of said prop-
107 erty since the issuing of this policy, by whom and for what
108 purpose any building herein described and the several parts
109 thereof were occupied at the time of loss and whether or not it
110 then stood on leased ground, and shall furnish a copy of all the
111 descriptions and schedules in all policies and, if required, verified
112 plans and specifications of any building, fixtures or machinery
113 destroyed or damaged. The insured, as often as may be reason-
114 ably required, shall exhibit to any person designated by this
115 Company all that remains of any property herein described, and
116 submit to examinations under oath by any person named by this
117 Company, and subscribe the same; and, as often as may be
118 reasonably required, shall produce for examination all books of
119 account, bills, invoices and other vouchers, or certified copies
120 thereof if originals be lost, at such reasonable time and place as
121 may be designated by this Company or its representative, and
122 shall permit extracts and copies thereof to be made.
123 Appraisal. In case the insured and this Company shall
124 fail to agree as to the actual cash value or
125 the amount of loss, then, on the written demand of either, each
126 shall select a competent and disinterested appraiser and notify
127 the other of the appraiser selected within twenty days of such
128 demand. The appraisers shall first select a competent and dis-

50 provisions. exist, or waiver of any provision be valid, unless granted herein or expressed in writing
52 added hereto. No provision, stipulation or forfeiture shall be
53 held to be waived by any requirement or proceeding on the part
54 of this Company relating to appraisal or to any examination
55 provided for herein.
56 Cancellation This policy shall be cancelled at any time
57 of policy. at the request of the insured, in which case
58 this Company shall, upon demand and sur-
59 render of this policy, refund the excess of paid premium above
60 the customary short rates for the expired time. This pol-
61 icy may be cancelled at any time by this Company by giving
62 to the insured a five days' written notice of cancellation with
63 or without tender of the excess of paid premium above the pro
64 rata premium for the expired time, which excess, if not ten-
65 dered, shall be refunded on demand. Notice of cancellation shall
66 state that said excess premium (if not tendered) will be re-
67 funded on demand.
68 Mortgage If loss hereunder is made payable, in whole
69 interests and or in part, to a designated mortgagee not
70 obligations. named herein as the insured, such interest in
71 this policy may be cancelled by giving to such
72 mortgage a ten days' written notice of can-
73 cellation.
74 If the insured fails to render proof of loss such mortgage, upon
75 notice, shall render proof of loss in the form herein specified
76 within sixty (60) days thereafter and shall be subject to the pro-
77 visions hereof relating to appraisal and time of payment and of
78 bringing suit. If this Company shall claim that no liability ex-
79 isted as to the mortgagor or owner, it shall, to the extent of pay-
80 ment of loss to the mortgagee, be subrogated to all the mort-
81 gagee's rights of recovery, but without impairing mortgagee's
82 right to sue; or it may pay off the mortgage debt and require
83 an assignment thereof and of the mortgage. Other provisions

132 the state in which the property covered is located. The ap-
133 praisers shall then appraise the loss, stating separately actual
134 cash value and loss to each item; and, failing to agree, shall
135 submit their differences, only, to the umpire. An award in writ-
136 ing, so itemized, of any two when filed with this Company shall
137 determine the amount of actual cash value and loss. Each
138 appraiser shall be paid by the party selecting him and the ex-
139 penses of appraisal and umpire shall be paid by the parties
140 equally.
141 Company's It shall be optional with this Company to
142 options. take all, or any part, of the property at the
143 agreed or appraised value, and also to re-
144 pair, rebuild or replace the property destroyed or damaged with
145 other of like kind and quality within a reasonable time, on giv-
146 ing notice of its intention so to do within thirty days after the
147 receipt of the proof of loss herein required.
148 Abandonment. There can be no abandonment to this Com-
149 pany of any property.
150 When loss The amount of loss for which this Company
151 payable. may be liable shall be payable sixty days
152 after proof of loss, as herein provided, is
153 received by this Company and ascertainment of the loss is made
154 either by agreement between the insured and this Company ex-
155 pressed in writing or by the filing with this Company of an
156 award as herein provided.
157 Suit. No suit or action on this policy for the recov-
158 ery of any claim shall be sustainable in any
159 court of law or equity unless all the requirements of this policy
160 shall have been complied with, and unless commenced within
161 twelve months next after inception of the loss.
162 Subrogation. This Company may require from the insured
163 an assignment of all right of recovery against
164 any party for loss to the extent that payment therefor is made
165 by this Company.

IN WITNESS WHEREOF, this Company has executed and attested these presents; but this policy shall not be valid unless counter-signed by the duly authorized Agent of this Company at the agency hereinbefore mentioned.

Secretary

President

ATTACH FORM BELOW THIS LINE

EXTENDED COVERAGE ENDORSEMENT NO. 4 Form ....

(PERILS OF WINDSTORM, HAIL, EXPLOSION, RIOT, RIOT ATTENDING A STRIKE, CIVIL COMMOTION, AIRCRAFT, VEHICLES, SMOKE, EXCEPT AS HEREINAFTER PROVIDED)

In consideration of the premium for this coverage shown on the first page of this policy, and subject to provisions and stipulations (hereinafter referred to as "provisions") herein and in the policy to which this endorsement is attached, including endorsements thereon, the coverage of this policy is extended to include direct loss by **Windstorm, Hail, Explosion, Riot, Riot Attending a Strike, Civil Commotion, Aircraft, Vehicles, and Smoke.**

This endorsement does not increase the amount or amounts of insurance provided in the policy to which it is attached.

If this policy covers on two or more items, the provisions of this endorsement shall apply to each item separately.

Substitution of Terms: In the application of the provisions of this policy, including endorsements (but not this endorsement), to the perils insured against by this Extended Coverage Endorsement, wherever the word "fire" appears there shall be substituted therefor the peril involved or the loss caused thereby, as the case requires.

Apportionment Clause: This Company shall not be liable for a greater proportion of any loss from any peril or perils included in this endorsement than (1) the amount of insurance under this policy bears to the whole amount of fire insurance covering the property, whether collectible or not, and whether or not such other fire insurance covers against the additional peril or perils insured hereunder; (2) nor for a greater proportion than the amount hereby insured bears to all insurance, whether collectible or not, covering in any manner such loss; except if any type of insurance other than fire with extended coverage or windstorm insurance applies to any loss to which this insurance also applies, the limit of liability of each type of insurance for such loss, hereby designated as "joint loss," shall first be determined as if it were the only insurance, and this type of insurance shall be liable for no greater proportion of joint loss than the limit of its liability for such loss bears to the sum of all such limits. The liability of this Company (under this endorsement) for such joint loss shall be limited to its proportionate part of the aggregate limit of this and all other insurance of the same type.

The words "joint loss," as used in the foregoing, mean that portion of the loss in excess of the highest deductible, if any, to which this endorsement and other types of insurance above referred to both apply.

War Risk Exclusion Clause: This Company shall not be liable for loss caused directly or indirectly by (a) hostile or warlike action in time of peace or war, including action in hindering, combating or defending against an actual, impending or expected attack, (1) by any government or sovereign power (de jure or de facto), or by any authority maintaining or using military, naval or air forces; or (2) by military, naval or air forces; or (3) by an agent of any such government, power, authority or forces, it being understood that any discharge, explosion or use of any weapon of war employing atomic fission or radioactive force shall be conclusively presumed to be such a hostile or warlike action by such a government, power, authority or forces; (b) insurrection, rebellion, revolution, civil war, usurped power, or action taken by governmental authority in hindering, combating or defending against such an occurrence.

Waiver of Policy Provisions: A claim for loss from perils included in this endorsement shall not be barred because

Loss Deductible Clause: It is a condition of this Extended Coverage Endorsement, that, in accordance with the provisions hereinafter contained, the sum of Fifty Dollars ($50.00) shall be deducted from the amount of loss resulting from each windstorm or hailstorm. This condition shall apply separately to each building or structure and separately to personal property in the open. This Loss Deductible Clause does not apply to contents contained in any building described herein.

This Company shall be liable for its proportion of the loss in excess of Fifty Dollars ($50.00) deducted in accordance with the apportionment provisions of this Extended Coverage Endorsement.

Provisions Applicable Only to Windstorm and Hail: This Company shall not be liable (1) for loss caused directly or indirectly by (a) frost or cold weather, or (b) ice (other than hail), sleet, snowstorm, waves, tide, tidal wave, high water, overflow of streams or bodies of water, or spray therefrom, all whether driven by wind or not; (2) for loss to the interior of the building(s) or the property covered therein caused by rain, snow, sand, or dust, whether driven by wind or not, unless the building(s) covered or containing the property covered shall first sustain an actual damage to roof or walls by the direct force of wind or hail and then shall be liable for loss to the interior of the building(s) or the property covered therein as may be caused by rain, snow, sand, or dust entering the building(s) through openings in the roof or walls made by direct action of wind or hail; (3) for loss to lawns, trees, shrubs and plants, or to outdoor radio and television antennas and aerials including their lead-in wiring, masts and towers; or (4) for loss by water from sprinkler equipment or other piping, unless such equipment or piping be damaged as a direct result of wind or hail.

Unless liability therefor is specifically assumed by endorsement to this Extended Coverage Endorsement, this Company shall not be liable for damage to the following property; (a) grain, hay, straw or other crops outside of buildings or (b) windmills, windpumps or their towers, or (c) crop silos (or their contents).

Provisions Applicable Only to Explosion: Loss by explosion shall include direct loss resulting from the explosion of accumulated gases or unconsumed fuel within the firebox (or combustion chamber) of any fired vessel or within the flues or passages which conduct the gases of combustion therefrom. However, this Company shall not be liable for loss by explosion, rupture or bursting of:

(a) steam boilers steam pipes, steam turbines or steam engines; or
(b) rotating parts of machinery caused by centrifugal force;

if owned by, leased by or actually operated under the control of the Insured.

The following are not explosions within the intent or meaning of these provisions:

(a) Concussion unless caused by explosion.
(b) Electrical arcing,
(c) Water hammer,
(d) Rupture or bursting of water pipes.

Any other explosion clause made a part of this policy is superseded by this endorsement.

(Provisions and Standard Clauses continued on reverse side.)

119

(Provisions and Standard Clauses, continued)

Provisions Applicable Only to Riot, Riot Attending a Strike and Civil Commotion: Loss by riot, riot attending a strike or civil commotion shall include direct loss by acts of striking employees of the owner or tenant(s) of the described building(s) while occupied by said striking employees and shall also include direct loss from pillage and looting occurring during and at the immediate place of a riot, riot attending a strike or civil commotion. Unless specifically endorsed hereon in writing this Company shall not be liable, however, for loss resulting from damage to or destruction of the described property owing to change in temperature or interruption of operations whether or not such loss is covered by this policy as to other perils.

Provisions Applicable Only to Loss by Aircraft and Vehicles: The term "vehicles," as used in this endorsement, means vehicles running on land or tracks but not aircraft. Loss by aircraft or by vehicles shall include only direct loss resulting from actual physical contact of an aircraft or a vehicle with the property covered hereunder or with the building containing the property covered hereunder, except that loss by aircraft includes direct loss by objects falling therefrom. This Company shall not be liable, however, for loss (a) by any vehicle owned or operated by the insured or by any tenant of the described premises; (b) by any vehicle to fences, driveways, walks or lawns; (c) to any aircraft or vehicle including contents thereof other than stocks of aircraft or vehicles in process of manufacture or for sale.

Provisions Applicable Only to Smoke: The term "smoke" as used in this endorsement means only smoke due to a sudden, unusual and faulty operation of any heating or cooking unit, only when such unit is connected to a chimney by a smoke pipe or by a vent, and while in or on the premises described in this policy, excluding, however, smoke from fireplaces or industrial apparatus.

Provisions Applicable Only when this Endorsement is attached to a Policy Covering Business Interruption, Tuition Fees, Extra Expense, Additional Living Expense, Rents, Leasehold Interest, Profits and Commissions or Consequential Loss: When this endorsement is attached to a policy covering Business Interruption, Tuition Fees, Extra Expense, Additional Living Expense, Rents, Leasehold Interest, Profits and Commissions, or Consequential Loss, the term "direct," as applied to loss, means loss, as limited and conditioned in such policy, resulting from direct loss to described property from perils insured against; and, while the business of the owner or tenant(s) of the described building(s) is interrupted by a strike at the described location, this Company shall not be liable for any loss owing to interference by any person(s) with rebuilding, repairing or replacing the property damaged or destroyed or with the resumption or continuation of business.

The provisions of the Loss Deductible Clause contained in this endorsement do not apply to insurance covering Business Interruption, Tuition Fees, Extra Expense, Additional Living Expense, Rents, Leasehold Interest, Profits and Commissions or Errors and Omissions.

CAUTION: When this Endorsement is attached to one fire policy, the insured should secure like coverage on all fire policies covering the same property.

120

ADDITIONAL EXTENDED
COVERAGE ENDORSEMENT

ADDITIONAL EXTENDED COVERAGE ENDORSEMENT

($50.00 DEDUCTIBLE CLAUSE AS HEREINAFTER PROVIDED)

Note: For use only with Extended Coverage Endorsement covering private dwelling property or contents thereof.

SECTION 1

In consideration of the premium for this coverage shown on the first page of this policy, and subject to the provisions of this policy of fire insurance and the Extended Coverage Endorsement attached thereto and of this endorsement, coverage is hereby extended to include direct loss by the PERILS INSURED AGAINST as set forth in the following provisions:

PROVISIONS

SECTION 2

PERILS INSURED AGAINST

THE ITALICIZED LETTERS FOLLOWING EACH PERIL REFER TO APPLICABLE PARAGRAPHS OF SECTION 3 (LIMITATIONS AND EXCLUSIONS).

AS SET FORTH IN SECTION 1, THIS POLICY IS EXTENDED TO COVER DIRECT LOSS CAUSED BY:

1. **Accidental discharge, leakage or overflow of water or steam** from within a plumbing, heating or air conditioning system or a domestic appliance (including necessary tearing out and replacing of any part of the building covered). *(A, B, C, D, E)*

2. **Sudden and accidental tearing asunder, cracking, burning or bulging of a steam or hot water heating or storage system** in the described building(s) caused by pressure of water or steam therein or by a deficiency of water

SECTION 3

LIMITATIONS AND EXCLUSIONS

THIS COMPANY SHALL NOT BE LIABLE:

(A) **As respects Perils 1, 2, 3, 4, 5, 6, 7, 8, 9 and 10:** ($50.00 LOSS DEDUCTIBLE CLAUSE) For loss by any one occurrence covered by this endorsement to the extent of Fifty Dollars ($50.00) and this Company is liable for loss in excess thereof [or, if there be other insurance, for its pro rata share of the loss in excess of Fifty Dollars ($50.00)]. If this policy covers on two or more items, this provision shall apply to each item separately.

(B) **As respects Perils 1, 2, 3, 4, 5, 6, 7, 8, 9 and 10:** For loss caused directly or indirectly by (a) earthquake, (b) backing up of sewers or drains, or (c) by flood, inundation, waves, tide or tidal wave, high water, or overflow of

3. Vandalism and malicious mischief, being only willful and malicious damage to or destruction of the described property, and including damage to the building(s) covered hereunder caused by burglars. (*A, B, E, F, G*)

4. Vehicles owned or operated **by the Insured** or by a tenant of the described premises, resulting from actual physical contact of such a vehicle with property covered hereunder or with the building containing property covered hereunder. (*A, B, G*)

5. Fall of trees or limbs, including their felling, topping or trimming. (*A, B, G*)

6. Objects falling from the weight of ice, snow or sleet. (*A, B, G*)

7. Freezing of plumbing, heating and air conditioning systems and domestic appliances. (*A, B, D*)

8. Collapse of building(s) or any part thereof, including collapse caused by weight of ice, snow or sleet. (*A, B, G, H*)

9. Landslide. (*A, B, G, H*)

10. Breakage of glass constituting a part of the describe building(s) covered hereunder, including glass in storm sash and storm windows. (*A, B, E*)

(C) **As respects Peril 1:** For the cost of repairing or replacing the plumbing, heating or air conditioning systems or domestic appliances, or parts thereof.

(D) **As respects Perils 1, 2 and 7:** For loss resulting from freezing while the described building(s) is vacant or unoccupied, unless the Insured shall have exercised due diligence with respect to maintaining heat in the building(s) or unless the plumbing, heating or air conditioning systems and domestic appliances had been drained and the water supply shut off during such vacancy or unoccupancy.

(E) **As respects Perils 1, 3 and 10:** For loss, if the described property had been vacant beyond a period of thirty (30) consecutive days immediately preceding the loss. A building in process of construction shall not be deemed vacant.

(F) **As respects Peril 3:** For loss by pilferage, theft, burglary or larceny.

(G) **As respects Perils 3, 4, 5, 6, 8 and 9:** For loss to outdoor equipment, fences, driveways, walks, lawns, trees, shrubs and plants, or retaining walls and bulkheads not constituting a part of a building covered.

(H) **As respects Perils 8 and 9:** For loss resulting from subsidence.

CAUTION

WHEN THIS ENDORSEMENT IS ATTACHED TO ONE FIRE-EXTENDED COVERAGE ENDORSEMENT POLICY, THE INSURED SHOULD SECURE LIKE COVERAGE ON ALL FIRE-EXTENDED COVERAGE ENDORSEMENT POLICIES COVERING THE SAME PROPERTY.

(End of Form)

123

Index

1666

London's fire led Dr. Nicolas Barbon to open first fire insurance office in historic venture one year later

1680

Coffee house owned by Edward Lloyd became a meeting place for shippers and others who sought insurance protection

1792

First American fire and marine insurance company was organized in room where Declaration of Independence was signed

1807

First insurance agent was appointed at Lexington, Kentucky, inaugurating personal service to policyholders in every community